How to Mend a Broken Heart

Also by Christine Webber

Get the Happiness Habit
Get the Self-Esteem Habit

How to Mend a Broken Heart

Christine Webber

HELP YOURSELF

British Library Cataloguing in Publication Data
A record for this book is available from the British Library

ISBN 0 340 86197 5

Typeset in ACaslonRegular by Avon DataSet Ltd,
Bidford-on-Avon, Warwickshire

Printed and bound in Great Britain by
Bookmarque Ltd, Croydon, Surrey

The paper and board used in this paperback are natural recyclable products
made from wood grown in sustainable forests. The manufacturing processes
conform to the environmental regulations of the country of origin.

Hodder & Stoughton
A Division of Hodder Headline Ltd
338 Euston Road
London NW1 3BH
www.madaboutbooks.com

To dearest David – my heart's desire

Contents

Acknowledgements

My special thanks go to Judith Longman at Hodder. This is our third book together and I truly value our working relationship and the friendship that has grown out of it.

I am also very grateful to Ali Gunn and Douglas Kean, my agents at Curtis Brown.

I am indebted to Dr Jack Dominian, whose work and ideas on genuine and authentic love have greatly influenced my own.

I'd also like to thank my two researchers, Susannah Pearce and Alex Webber, for all their dependable effort.

And finally I say a big 'thank-you' to all the people – patients, friends, relatives and colleagues – whose experiences have found their way into these pages. All names have been changed and all details have been camouflaged to mask everyone's real identity.

Part One

Accepting It

1

Accepting and Understanding Your Pain

Having a broken heart is hell. It's the worst pain in the world. It's also:

- the loneliest feeling;
- the scariest sensation;
- isolating;
- devastating.

It addition, it frequently makes you doubt your own sanity – and leaves you feeling that life is pointless, hopeless and over.

No wonder heroines in Victorian novels and romantic operas often die of 'the condition'. But dying is the easy option. It's *living* with a broken heart that's difficult.

Difficult, did I say? That's an understatement if ever there was one. Difficult? It's far worse than that. It's dreadful, tough, ghastly, seemingly endless and *almost* impossible to deal with – that's the really important word: almost. It feels impossible, but it's not. Millions of people could tell you their story of how – eventually – their broken heart was mended.

Your heart, too, will mend. It just doesn't seem like it right now.

We can feel broken-hearted in many different situations:

- when love is unrequited;
- when first love ends;
- when a marriage or long-term relationship ends;
- when we're dumped;
- when we do the dumping;
- when a clandestine affair comes to an end;
- when our own behaviour ruins a relationship;
- when a partner dies;
- when a close friend dies;
- when a loved relative dies;
- when a pet dies;
- when we lose a job that has meant everything to us.

These are twelve appallingly awful situations. You might be surprised by the last five of them – involving death and job loss – but I must say immediately that I am not going to cover them in any detail; after all, there are already many books which deal with death and bereavement, and plenty of others which help readers cope with job loss. These situations are on the list because they usually evoke extremely upsetting emotions – and cause heartbreak – and also because much of the advice in this book will also help people who are suffering from them.

Perhaps the toughest heartbreak is your very first one. Despite all the statistics to the contrary, many of us believe that our first love will endure. That first time, we may be so in love that we simply cannot imagine a time when those feelings will disappear, or stop being reciprocated.

First love is so delicious. So 'heady'. So exciting. We usually start thinking about making a family with this new and perfect person. A golden life stretches before us. Our love is different. Our love is here to stay.

Alas, all too often it isn't.

On the very day that I started writing this book, I received the following email at the NetDoctor website where I answer users' questions on sex and relationships. It was from a young man:

> I just wanted to know if you had advice for a broken heart? My girlfriend was such an awesome, beautiful person that I can't stop loving her. She just decided one day that she was falling out of love with me, and had feelings for another boy. I know I have a lot to learn about love and life – but I was so sure that she was the girl that would be my wife someday. How can I accept that she doesn't love me and move on with my life? How can I ever let myself love again? I just don't understand why this all happened. If you have any advice at all it would be greatly appreciated. Thank you.

I almost wept when I read it. In fact, you'd have to be made of stone not to feel this nineteen-year-old's pain. And I guess that most people who read his email will sigh – not only for him, but also in memory of that first, worst nightmare of their own.

The other really awful thing about it is that he is obviously so nice. In the midst of his anguish, he is sweetly polite and grateful – which somehow makes his query all the more poignant.

This email raises a very important truth – and it may well help you to try to accept it right now. It is this: *Terrible things happen to really lovely people.*

That seems very unfair and cruel, doesn't it? In fact, it flies in the face of most of what we learned as children. We've all been led to understand that goodness gets its own reward.

Our parents told us: 'If you're good, you'll get that computer for Christmas.' 'If you're a nice, quiet boy for half an hour, Mummy will read you a story later.' 'If you eat up your cabbage, you'll grow up to be big and strong.' 'If you work hard at school, you'll pass your exams and be able to go to university/get a good job.'

Of course, much of the time, being good or wise or hard-working *does* reap a genuine reward. So when we give love, and put a lot of effort into a relationship, and then it goes wrong, this disaster seems to break all our rules and assumptions about life. It feels very unfair. And it is.

In fact, for many of us, it's the first time that we come face to face with the unpalatable fact that life often *is* unfair and that there are no guarantees.

A broken heart is a huge drama when we're young – but it can also be dreadfully painful later in life. Nowadays, we enjoy such fluid, flexible lifestyles – we live longer, change careers several times, move around the country (or even abroad) – that it can be quite common for us to have several highly significant relationships in our lives. And each time one ends, there's likely to be some heartbreak.

Does it get easier? In one sense, perhaps it does. We know we got over it before – eventually. But heartbreak can still be a monumental blow, particularly when we had thought we were 'settled' for life.

Looking back at my own history, I realise that I've felt truly broken-hearted about three times – and I think the third was the worst. I had invested so much in that particular relationship: it had seemed to be everything that I had never had before. And I simply could not see how anything better could ever happen again.

Of course it *did* and I eventually became happier than I could have dared to hope. But in retrospect, I realise that one of the things that made my heartache so difficult to recover from was the fact that I was thinking about it the wrong way. In other words, it wasn't just the situation that caused me such suffering, but rather my own thoughts.

This might seem an odd concept to you right now, but as you work through this book, you'll understand what I mean. And you'll also come to realise that your present thoughts are not helping *you*.

You see, in the crisis of a broken heart, we tend to become

illogical – and that makes things worse. We say, or think, 'I'm really, really desperate and hurting and upset and forlorn . . .'

All these things are true. But what we go on to think or say is: '. . . and I will never love again, and no one will ever love me again, and life is going to be absolutely dreadful for ever.'

Does this sound like you? It certainly sounds like I used to be! But can you see that while it's true that you're feeling desperate and hurting and upset and forlorn, it *isn't* accurate to state that you won't fall in love again, or that no one will ever love you, or indeed that your life is going to be absolutely dreadful for ever?

The fact is that even though you've lost a great love, there is no earthly reason why you should not love again, or be loved, or that your life should be perpetually horrid. You don't have a crystal ball, or any other means of looking into the future, so you can't possibly *know* those things. But by thinking them, or saying them to yourself, you are making yourself feel very much more wretched than you need be.

So here's the first bit of advice to get you on the road to recovery:

Try to stop making wild predictions about the future – and concentrate instead on getting through the awfulness of the present.

Your current predicament is quite tough enough. So try not to mentally condemn yourself to a lousy future – because if you do, you're making everything harder than it needs to be.

This book is designed to be used – and worked through – over several months. Of course, you may, in your need and desire to make things better, read it from cover to cover in a matter of hours. If you do, my advice is that you then start at the beginning again, and work on each section piece by piece.

I have tried to look at this problem from many different angles and if you're going to get your money's worth, I strongly urge you not to skip bits, but to work on all the chapters in turn.

To recover fully, you need to take care of yourself and to examine what your broken relationship was *really* like.

7

You'll also benefit from investigating what you're thinking – and working out whether your thoughts are helping or hindering you. Then it will help if you assess what you want from the rest of your life. Then finally, you'll be ready to rebuild your social and romantic life.

All these things are covered in the pages that follow. But obviously you can't master them all overnight! So, take your time, and try to be patient.

If you can work on all these facets of your heartbreak, slowly and thoroughly, then you'll not only feel much better, but you'll also become a stronger and much more healthy person mentally. And best of all, you should never have to suffer so badly ever again.

2

Care, Support and Getting in Touch with Your Own Goodness

So the worst has happened. Your heart is broken. This may have happened very recently, or perhaps you've been struggling with these feelings for many months.

In this part of the book, I'm going to help you to accept that your relationship is over, that you feel dreadful, that you need help in getting over it – and that you must take care of yourself.

And that's where we're going to start.

Caring for Yourself

If your heartbreak is recent, you probably haven't yet got round to nurturing yourself properly and to caring for yourself through this crisis.

And if your heartbreak happened a while ago, but is still really painful, maybe you *never* went through this period of nurture and care and acceptance, and perhaps this is one of the reasons why your pain is still so raw.

Caring for yourself is a vital part of your recovery, so no matter how long you've been suffering, try from today to start looking after yourself with kindness and love.

Some of this care will involve diet and nurture of your body, and some will involve care of your emotions, but both kinds of care are equally important.

If you have a broken heart, you're likely to feel lousy about yourself. If you've chosen to end a marriage or a relationship, you're probably feeling mean, horrible, selfish and frightened. And if you've been bereaved, or dumped, then doubtless you're feeling bleak, unloved, unlovable and unlovely.

Whatever set of emotions you're experiencing, it's unlikely that you feel very proud of yourself right now, or that you regard yourself highly, or feel that you're a very deserving person.

Caring for your body and your mind will help you to regain positive feelings about yourself, because every time you do something loving, kind and nurturing for *you*, you will reinforce a very important message – which is that you are a unique, worthwhile and wonderful individual.

To care for yourself properly, you need to accept that you are (or have been) in a state of shock – even if you anticipated your current heartbreak.

It might help to compare the end of your relationship with a situation where someone is nursing a relative up till his or her death. They talk about the end, they expect the end, they may even long for the end, so that the loved one will have no more pain, but they're still shocked when that end comes.

The same is true of the demise of a relationship. So, no matter how your heartbreak came about, please accept that you're a victim of shock – and treat yourself accordingly.

Let me tell you about Anna. She was a woman in her thirties who had married for all the wrong reasons. Even before her marriage, her relationship was always very hard work, but, like many women, she had been worried that if she didn't marry this man, no one else would ask her.

The marriage was not a success. Her husband was work-shy

and moody and a champion 'couch potato'. In the face of his inadequacies, Anna gradually became the chief organiser and breadwinner.

Over a period of ten years, her confidence grew – and so did her resentment that all the work in maintaining the marriage was done by her. Even so, she clung on in there, hoping against hope that her marriage could work and that one day – with her love and encouragement – her husband would change for the better.

He didn't. Eventually, her patience ran out and she ended the relationship. She had longed for this day of freedom. In fact, for at least five years, she had been plucking up courage to call 'time' on this hopeless partnership. But when she finally did it, she couldn't stop crying – great splashy teardrops and gut-wrenching sobs.

Despite her emotional state, she went to work the next day – she was by now a very successful businesswoman – but her secretary took one look at her and bundled her into a taxi and sent her to her mother's house.

'I'm really glad I've ended it,' she told her parents – who were massively relieved to be shot of their hopeless son-in-law. But even while she was insisting how glad she was, she continued to weep. What was she crying for? Was her heart broken? You might not think so – especially if you've recently been dumped by someone and feel that Anna, having ended her marriage of her own volition, had no right to be sad.

But Anna *was* sad. Incredibly sad. And she was crying because her heart *was* broken. She didn't want her husband back. But she was heartbroken because:

- she'd wasted time;
- she'd picked the wrong guy;
- she was ten years older than she'd been when she'd got involved with him;
- she had no children;
- her hopes and dreams had come nothing.

Anna was in shock, even though she had been the one to end the marriage. Fortunately, her mother understood what Anna was going through and put her to bed and provided her with lots of that most British of shock treatments – hot, sweet tea! And this was the beginning of her long, slow process to recovery.

But it isn't just women who fall apart when a relationship ends. I've had plenty of devastated and heartbroken men in my consulting room too. One, whom I'll call Gary, was trembling so violently when he first came to me that he could hardly walk; and when I gave him a cup of coffee, his hands shook so much that he could barely raise the cup to his lips. He cried a lot, and his breathing sounded painful and erratic. In fact, had I met him out on the street, and not known why he was in such a terrible state, I would have assumed that he was a heroin addict in need of a 'fix'.

So, heartbreak is certainly not the sole preserve of the fairer sex. It can happen just as easily to blokes.

As it happens, most of my heartbroken male patients have been heterosexual, but let us not forget that gay men and women also frequently fall in love very romantically and powerfully – and can feel utterly distraught at the end of a relationship.

So, whatever your sexual orientation, and whatever has caused your heartbreak, it's highly likely that you're experiencing shock. And you need to *treat* this shock in order for your broken heart to be able to start to mend.

The best way to tackle this is to try to imagine how you would want to look after someone else – someone very special in your life – who had had major surgery, or a terrible car smash. You'd want to get them plenty of rest, feed them healthy but delicious food and provide them with books or videos that would cheer them up. You might also spoil them with thoughtful gifts that would help the nurturing process – such as body lotion, or a herb pillow, or a visit to an aromatherapist.

Whatever you'd do for someone else in this kind of situation is exactly what you should now be doing for yourself. So, if you're numb with mental and physical cold, keep warm and cosy; if you're upset and feeling shaky, take plenty of rest; if you're feeling rejected and unwanted, do things for yourself that make you feel better – such as walking by the sea, or having a long, scented bath by candlelight; if your appetite has gone, tempt your palate with little treats that you might not normally allow yourself; and if you're eating a load of junk food for comfort – such as burgers and chocolate – make sure that you're also eating five portions of fruit or vegetables a day and drinking at least eight glasses of water. That way, you'll get the satisfaction of knowing that you're doing *something* decent for yourself and your body. If you carry on with a diet consisting solely of junk food, or too much alcohol, coffee or cigarettes, you will compound your sense of being a failure and not worth bothering with.

Another important factor is exercise. You may be so distressed that all you can do is sit on the sofa and cry. But try to get out of the house at least once a day so that you can fill your lungs with fresh air. Even a quick walk to the shops can start to help you feel fitter, and should elevate your spirits.

You should also allow time every day to pamper yourself. Even the most macho of guys can soak in a fragrant bath, while listening to favourite music – and begin to feel better. And most women not only enjoy soaking in the bath, but also feel a greater sense of love and care for their own body if they massage in some body lotion afterwards.

Caring acts like these remind you that you are special, even if your heart is telling you that nothing matters any more.

Sleep, too, is a great healer when you're broken-hearted, but unfortunately, though some people sleep a lot when they're distressed, others find sleep at such times very elusive. Some of these individuals can't actually *fall* asleep. Others can go off to sleep easily enough, but wake up in the empty, bleak hours before dawn, and stay awake.

If you are wakeful in the night, don't toss and turn in bed. Get up and make yourself a milky drink. Read a book that's an old favourite, or watch a video that will cheer you in some way.

But what if your insomnia gets worse and you're getting so little sleep that you're becoming more upset and unable to cope with a routine day? First of all, although you may be tempted to use alcohol as a sedative, try to avoid it. It produces rather unnatural and fitful sleep, and increasing your dependence on booze at a time like this is never helpful. There are several common herbal remedies that promote slumber, and these are definitely worth trying. You can get them from chemists or health-food stores.

But what if your sleep patterns still don't improve? And what if you're so tired you don't feel able to work? Or what should you do if you are so miserable that you stop looking after yourself, or functioning in any normal way? Should you go and seek medical help?

Yes, you should. I should point out, however, that although you probably feel that you've got a dead weight in your chest – and although in some languages the term for a 'broken heart' is the same as that of a 'heart attack' – the truth is that there's nothing physically wrong with your heart. Furthermore, the loss of a relationship is not a medical condition, and some individuals treat it as such rather too readily. One Sussex GP told me of a woman who had dumped her husband on a Saturday and was queuing up outside the doctor's surgery on the Monday for anti-depressants.

Now, of course the end of a relationship, or the death of someone close – or even the death of a pet, or the loss of a job – will seriously upset you and can cause desperate misery. But this is *normal*. We *ought* to be sad when something bad happens. That's life. And that's the time when we have to treat ourselves as though we were an invalid and lean on other people.

But if, after several days or weeks of shock and distress, you're really not functioning, you can't stop crying, you don't feel able to leave the house, you're not sleeping, or you feel so devastated that you're considering suicide, then, very definitely, you must see a doctor. Quite apart from anything else, you might need a doctor to sign you off work for a while: few of us are much use to our employers while we're in this kind of a state.

Doctors are generally sympathetic to the problems surrounding the end of a relationship and will usually do their best to help. It would be wise to ask for a double slot when making an appointment to see your GP. This will ensure that he or she has adequate time to allow you to unburden yourself.

Your doctor may possibly give you a prescription for some sleeping pills. You might be worried about this and wonder if you'll get hooked on them, which will merely add to your already considerable problems. But if you just take them for a very brief period, or only occasionally, you won't run into problems of addiction – and you will also start coping better once you're no longer so fatigued.

Some doctors will also offer tranquillisers for a short time – particularly if you've suffered *sudden* trauma like the death of someone close, or if your partner has just walked out with no warning.

Again, this medical help can be timely, but should definitely not be long-term. There's only so much good that can be achieved by wrapping yourself in a chemical haze to protect yourself from harsh and uncomfortable feelings. These feelings mostly have to be lived with and talked about if they are to be dealt with adequately.

And what about anti-depressants? These are of little help at the beginning of your distress. For a start, they won't immediately alter your mood because they usually take a couple of weeks to work. Secondly, the sadness you feel is not the same as clinical depression – at least not initially.

However, if your sadness goes on and on and makes your life really difficult – and if you can't derive any pleasure from things that would normally please you – then I do think there's a case for discussing anti-depressants with your GP.

However, in the early days of your heartbreak, the most important things you can do are to:

- talk to friends or family about how you feel;
- eat as healthily as possible – and tempt yourself with special treats;
- drink alcohol only sparingly;
- take some exercise;
- play music that you like – or even music that puts you in touch with your sorrowful feelings and makes you cry;
- get out of the house at least once a day;
- watch some videos – especially if you've got old films saved that you could never watch with your ex-partner because your tastes weren't similar;
- take plenty of scented baths;
- treat your body with love and kindness – perhaps go for a massage or aromatherapy session, and/or use fragrant emollients on your skin so that your body feels nurtured and cared for.

Allowing Other People to Support You

I've already suggested that when you're heartbroken it's vital to lean on your friends or close family. For some people this is the easy bit. Like Anna, they have a mother who wraps them in cotton wool and provides tea and sympathy and very soothing chicken soup!

But not all of us are blessed with relatives like Anna's. And of course sometimes we feel so distressed, or such a failure, that we don't feel able to cry on anyone's shoulder. It can be particularly difficult to open up to our friends or family if none of them approved of our relationship in the first place. It's also tough to admit to the end of a romance if you've already had a string of relationship failures.

And parents aren't always helpful. Let's say you have a

mother who blames you for not yet making her a granny. You're unlikely to want to confide in her if you're fearful that you're going to get a sermon about how hopeless you are, and how disappointed she is that you've 'failed' yet again.

Then, if you're gay, you're likely to have all sorts of other issues to deal with. If you're broken-hearted about the loss of your first same-gender romance, and your family were hostile to you 'coming out', they may choose to assume that you've now seen the error of your ways and that you're straight after all! And if they're bigoted and narrow-minded, they may even see your unhappiness as a rightful judgement on you.

Small wonder, then, that many people don't feel they want to lean on their families when the worst happens. And of course, seemingly tough and capable guys frequently have real difficulty in confiding in *anyone*. The chances are that their relationships with their mates centre on sport or drinking, and they can't see how they can possibly talk about how devastated they feel to any of them. Such blokes may also find it difficult to unburden themselves to their families – even the female members. Fortunately, many young males nowadays have platonic women friends who are usually good at providing female affirmation and sympathy, though some men are so buttoned-up emotionally that they can't talk to even them. This aversion to sharing sorrow is a big problem and can make their recovery a much lengthier and lonelier one.

I have, incidentally, known some individuals who have been so concerned with keeping up appearances that they have actually pretended that the split in their relationship hasn't happened. For instance, one woman whose new husband walked out soon after their marriage – a five-star affair with a huge marquee in the grounds of a country house, complete with designer presents and a Caribbean honeymoon – refused to tell anyone about the demise of the relationship. Instead, she pretended that her man had suddenly got the job of his dreams abroad. Unfortunately, it wasn't long before he was spotted – shopping for one in a Waitrose store!

Keeping your personal tragedy private will not help in the long run, so no matter how difficult it is for you, do find someone to confide in. This tends to be easier for women than for men, but everyone needs a shoulder to cry on.

In fact, you need a friend who will be there for you – or at least at the end of a phone – at all times. It's very common for your heart to ache most at three in the morning, and having someone who will be available to you, even at that hour, is the biggest of comforts.

So don't be secretive about your suffering. Let other people help you. It may hurt your pride, but it will heal your heart. And you may even make new friends through this bleakest of times. For example, there may be someone in your office whom you hardly know who has been through some similar trauma and becomes a real rock for you.

Of course, you may worry that you're being a nuisance, but I'm sure *you* would be a listening ear for one of your friends if he or she were in the same situation.

Also, the more you talk in the early days – and you can talk it out with several friends, not just one – the more quickly you'll recover.

Most pals will happily put up with you weeping all over them for at least a couple of months: but their patience may wear thin after six months or more, so make the most of the early days when sympathy is being extended to you. Allow other people to nurse you and cuddle you and take over your life. They want to help – and even if you're generally a very self-reliant person, this is the time to let them.

But what if your family is a long way away? Or what if you have no friends nearby? When distance is a problem, you can of course phone. But many people nowadays have email and use it to spill out their feelings. It may not be as good as face-to-face support, but it certainly beats not having any at all.

And what about a lack of friends? Very, very few people have no friends. These unfortunate individuals are generally without friends for a very good reason – which is that they've never realised that to *have* a friend you have to *be* one.

I doubt very much if any readers of this book are friendless. But if you are, let me just say that it isn't just your broken heart that needs mending, it's your whole attitude to life. Tough though it is, you need to start making a lot of changes, and perhaps now that you've suffered such a blow, you will.

But most of us *do* have friends. However, yours may not be very near you, and you may not have kept up with them as much as you'd have liked. You may have moved round the country because of your partner's job, and thus lost touch with school or college friends, or you may have had children and perhaps never quite made the time to keep up with old pals.

Your social circle might consist only of couples – people who know you as half of a pair – who are reluctant to take sides in your split. Or you may have been so unhappy during the dying months of the relationship that you shut yourself away and neglected all your friends. But somewhere in your past there will be warmth, love and concern flowing in your direction, so take a look around you. Spot who is on your side and who loves and wants to help you – and then let them.

Usually, part of the recovery process with our friends will involve us in learning about *their* past romantic history, and benefiting from finding out how they got over traumas such as you're experiencing now.

It's no bad thing to discover that, whatever we're going through, others have been through similar situations – or worse. It also helps to know that your suffering is not unique and that others have triumphed over heartbreak – even if, deep down, you suspect that no one has ever been quite so cruelly rejected, or so publicly humiliated, as you have!

Share these experiences, but most of all, talk about *you*. This will help you heal. As soon as we open up and share our pain and distress it immediately ceases to have such a powerful hold over us. So, get talking – and one day you'll realise that your story has become boring, not just to others, but to yourself as well! And then you'll be well on the way to recovery.

Nowadays, there are also support organisations where you can share what's happened to you with other people. Two of the best are excellent associations for single people: Single Living and So You've Been Dumped.

For more details, see the Help Yourself Directory at the back of the book.

Getting in Touch with Your Own Goodness

Learning to lean on other people may be very hard for some adults – as we've seen. But it becomes easier with practice, and I cannot stress how important it is.

However, talking to others – and letting them comfort us – is not the whole solution. We also need to open ourselves up to our own goodness.

When we're heartbroken, we tend to act like a hedgehog: we roll into an emotional ball which has forbidding spikes all over it. Allowing other people to penetrate our defences requires trust and love, but most of us get there eventually.

Unfortunately, even though we may gradually open ourselves up to the care and love of others, we often continue to feel very, very prickly. This is because we feel so desolate and so betrayed.

One of the ways we can become more open, more attractive – and feel more at peace with ourselves and others – is to become more aware of our own goodness: not only the good that we do, but also the goodness that is part of our basic nature.

You see, when we're heartbroken, we usually feel very down on ourselves. From time to time we get angry and might say things like: 'She just used me', or 'I did everything to make the relationship work', or even, 'None of this is my fault.' But even while we rail against the gods, the universe and our ex-partner, there's a small voice inside us telling us that we're no good, that we're hateful, and that it's no wonder we've ended up lonely and alone.

It's this small voice that needs sorting now. And the best way of doing so is to become aware of the good that you do. If you manage to smile at someone while standing in a queue, or you buy a small gift for someone who's been helping you, or you help a blind person across the road, take a moment and inwardly register that you've been kind and that you've done something good.

Also, persuade yourself that you must continue to see need in others. Often when we're really hurting, we stop watching the television news, and if we see an appeal for famine-struck Africa we turn over the page. We may also cross the street to avoid a *Big Issue* seller, or someone jingling a charity tin. I'm not suggesting that you can take on the world's problems – certainly not at present – but I am pressing you to be aware of other people's difficulties, even though you feel so very bound up in your own.

If you turn yourself into an island of hurt and hate, your recovery will be a very slow one. So, even in the midst of your own pain, try to extend to others the charity and generosity that exist inside you. When you do this, you'll feel better about yourself.

A very badly hurt patient of mine, whom I'll call Lizzie, had become closed off to her own good qualities. I tried talking to her about them but, whenever I did, she gave me a withering glance. However, she found out – all by herself – that uncovering your own goodness, and giving it expression, can be an enormous help.

Lizzie's birthday came three months after her boyfriend left her. She'd been dreading it; so much so that she refused to celebrate it, and, to keep out of her friends' way, she drove herself to the coast for the day, alone.

It was cold. The sun and sea looked grey and charmless and as she stomped along, she muttered angrily to herself that her life was a complete mess and that she was a total dead loss as a person.

On a windy corner near the seafront, she came upon an old guy playing a saxophone. She plodded on angrily, determined not to give him any money. But then, despite her bad mood, she found herself walking more jauntily in time to his rhythm.

Why was this talented man busking on a street corner, she wondered? Why were his clothes threadbare? What troubles in his life – relationships, drugs, drink – had brought him to this? She didn't know the answers to these questions. But what she *did* know was that his playing had penetrated the hostile barrier she'd erected around herself.

She went back, stopped and listened. Other people followed her example, and soon there was a crowd around him. He played several popular melodies, and soon people were clapping, singing along and smiling, even though it was such a foul day. Many of them dropped money in the guy's cap and when he finally stopped playing, Lizzie pressed twenty pounds into his hand and thanked him for his music.

As she walked away, she found herself crying. But the tears weren't her usual kind of sorrow and hurt and recrimination. Instead, they were something to do with the man's talent and how it had opened her up, and also about how her example had led to others stopping and supporting him and having a good time – so that the whole atmosphere in that small, windswept seaside town had improved.

Her heart, which she had thought was irreparably damaged, began to glow with a sense of achievement and an emotion approaching happiness. It was strange: she hadn't felt that way in months. Lizzie went into a café bar and ordered some food and a glass of wine – and she toasted herself and her future.

I'd like to tell you that from that moment on Lizzie lived happily ever after, but I'm not writing a fairy story – I'm writing about real people, with very real problems. However, what I *can* tell you is that although Lizzie still had plenty of obstacles to happiness to overcome, she began to improve dramatically from that day because she had been able to get herself back in touch with her own goodness.

Are you in touch with yours?

3

Acknowledging and Accepting Loss

After the shock of your heartbreak has begun to sink in, you have to learn to live with your loss. Your tears – if you're someone who has cried a lot – will be less frequent. Your numbness will thaw out. Your trembling will gradually cease. Your acute pain will dull into a pressing ache. But will you feel better?

No! In fact, you might decide that you feel *worse*. During your period of shock, you will have been in a state of disbelief. You will probably have felt that at any moment you would wake up from your nightmare and discover that it hadn't happened after all.

But, gradually, you will have accepted the truth of your situation. Indeed, you'll have become all too familiar with it – and then your sense of loss may well have become overwhelming.

It's at these times that you will keep thinking and telling yourself: *My life is never, ever going to be the same again.* This can be a hugely depressing thought and you'll probably feel that it threatens to engulf and destroy you – like a twenty-foot wave in a stormy sea. So I'm going to give you another thought that you should try to substitute for it, and it's this: *It's true that my life has changed. It's going to be very different. But 'different' need not mean 'worse'. In fact, my life may become better than it's ever been. Unfortunately, this won't happen overnight.* It will really help if you start thinking this way.

As I said in Chapter One, when something bad happens, it's all too easy to exaggerate the awfulness of the situation by telling yourself – and believing it – that nothing good, nice or wonderful can ever happen to you again. But it can. And it will.

However, before this can happen, you have to overcome your feelings of loss. And in order to do this, you may have to find some new perspectives.

Your greatest sense of loss at the moment is probably that you are no longer in a relationship that you would prefer to be in. Even if you ended it yourself, you've probably done so because it failed to live up to what you believe you needed – and you are having to face up to the loss of something that once seemed really promising.

But most people reading this book will be reading it because they have been rejected by a partner. And their loss will centre around the removal of the person they still loved and believed in. Perhaps, secretly, they may have realised that all was not well, but they still wanted to be *in* the relationship far more than they wanted to be *out* of it.

So, losing the relationship, and being without the person you thought was so special, is the Number One loss. But there are plenty of others. And I believe that in order to see the full reality of your past relationship, and then to move on, you first need to identify, acknowledge and accept all these various losses.

There may be the loss of a home. There could well be a big loss in income. For people who worked together, there could even be the loss of a job.

There is certainly the loss of 'being a couple'. And with it comes the loss of some mutual friends – usually other couples.

Many of these people will avoid you now, as they will be reluctant to take sides, or be fearful that your split will make their own relationship more vulnerable.

Some people feel a loss of status. Unfortunately, even today, there are individuals who identify themselves through their partner. So if you achieved your aim of marrying a politician, or a surgeon, or someone very wealthy – but now have been dumped – you may well feel that your status has plummeted. Or perhaps you feel that a single person has less standing in society than someone who is married, or cohabiting with a partner. This would definitely have been true fifty years ago. Personally, I think it no longer applies, but that doesn't stop some adults from feeling that way.

Other losses may revolve around the big gestures or big sacrifices we often make in order to try to save a failing relationship. It's very common, for example, for cohabiting couples whose relationship is in trouble to suddenly decide to marry, in a bid to make things better. Unfortunately, matrimony rarely solves relationship problems. And if everything finally falls apart shortly after this trip down the aisle, both partners can feel that they've not only fallen out of love, but also that they've lost their dignity as well. They may even sense that some of their acquaintances find their short-lived marriage quite comical – which is very hard to bear.

It's also not uncommon for a couple whose relationship is rocky to decide that having a baby will put things right. This is one of the worst reasons I know for parenthood, and yet it happens time and time again.

Breaking up after making a baby is a hugely painful loss. One of you will probably find that you become a 'bit-part player' in your child's life, and you will keenly feel the loss of the stable family that you wanted to offer your infant – as well as the loss of your romance.

Another great loss – and one that generates much distress and guilt – is termination. If a pregnancy happens when a relationship is not in the best of health, the couple may decide that their relationship can only survive if the woman has an abortion. Or, one partner may insist on termination as a condition of continuing the relationship. If that relationship then fails, there can be enormous sorrow and guilt about the abortion – and anger too. It's massively painful to realise that you've gone against your own wants, or beliefs, or needs, and sacrificed a new life for an old romance which then ends anyway.

So losses connected with forlorn gestures or compromises are especially difficult to come to terms with.

Then there are those losses that occur when people are desperate to have a family. There may have been a miscarriage – which is a dreadful loss at any time – but when that sadness accelerates the end of the relationship, it can feel like the end of the world.

And, sadly, may couples being treated for infertility find the strain of IVF or some similar treatment becomes so great that their relationship withers and dies.

In all these cases, the loss of parenthood on top of the loss of a partner augments the feelings of desolation.

Frequently, too, a couple who have stayed together 'for the children' might find that nothing binds them once the kids leave home. The end of a marriage or long-term relationship at that time can leave the woman, in particular, with the feeling that she is redundant, and that everything meaningful is lost.

Another type of loss that can be very isolating and miserable is when a clandestine affair comes to an end. As an agony aunt, I've always felt terribly sad whenever I received letters from women telling me that they'd been in an illicit affair for years: years when they were never able to publicly demonstrate their love, or even to spend birthdays or Christmas with the object of their devotion.

I felt even sadder when they wrote to tell me that the lover, who was so reluctant to upset his wife and leave home, eventually *did* leave – but for someone new rather than the mistress who had loved him so faithfully through the years.

Such a person – who is usually female, but not always – has to be very discreet about her grief, and can feel as though she has not only been robbed of her love but also of her past and future too, having never married, or had children. She is also likely to feel utterly discarded, and as if there is no sign or recognition anywhere of the fact that this important love actually existed. And of course, trying to get the necessary support after the split can be difficult if you never let your parents or many of your close friends know about the relationship in the first place. There is more about getting over an affair in Chapter Nine.

Nowadays, there's another type of secret relationship that has become quite common. It's when someone from one culture has been romantically linked to a person from another. Secret relationships like these are taking place all over Britain – especially in universities, hospitals, lawyers' offices and other places where a common education or training has brought together people of similar intellect and interests, but of different backgrounds.

Take Raj, for example. He's a Sikh doctor who was brought up and educated in Britain, and who has masses of friends from several different cultures. Raj's family are still very traditionalist and his father wants him to have an arranged marriage with someone from his own community. But Raj has his own ideas on romance and, some time ago, he fell in love with an Irish nurse called Maeve. Keeping his love secret from his parents, they set up home together.

Unfortunately, the secrecy caused problems. After months of being together, Maeve wanted him to tell his family about their relationship, while Raj begged her to accept that, for now, he felt he could not. Eventually, these stresses became too much and she dumped him and retired hurt to her family in Ireland.

Raj could not confide in his family and get love and support for his broken heart from them. He also shied away from telling his friends – especially his European ones – because he thought they would not understand his family pressures and would assume he should have stood up to his parents and done his own thing. But only someone in Raj's situation can fully understand how torn he felt between two ways of life.

Nowadays this is a common scenario. I personally see situations like this all the time. People like Raj, who have been brought up in the UK but who have parents who adhere strictly to their own traditions, can feel extraordinarily lost at this time. They feel estranged from their lover and alienated from their own culture, so that they don't quite feel 'at home' anywhere. Sometimes, having failed at their own handling of romance, they do go back to the family and allow them to arrange a marriage, hoping that if they go back to the 'fold' they'll feel more grounded and find peace and happiness.

If this applies to you, can I say that I *do* believe that you have a lot of thinking to do. I am certainly not saying that the modern way of doing things must be the best, but I think you should try to be true to:

- you, the person you started out as;
- you, the person you struggled to become;
- and you, the person you are now.

In other words, take your time. A sudden change of direction now – one way or the other – might only wreak more havoc in the long-term.

All the losses that we've looked at so far have occurred as a result of the end of the relationship. But looking back, you may start to realise that there were plenty of losses *within* it that you never fully acknowledged while you were together.

Perhaps your partner disliked your friends and family – and so consequently you saw them less and less often in a bid to keep the peace. You can feel very foolish – as well as very alone – when you then lose your partner.

Maybe you held yourself back in career terms because your partner wouldn't re-locate so that you could take up a promotion. Perhaps you feared that your success would scare off your loved one. Or possibly you abandoned your own job to support your spouse in some venture or other. Now you have nothing: neither the career success you could have had, nor the partner you sacrificed it for. No wonder you feel bleak and bereft.

You can also feel very cheated if you helped your partner through tough times in anticipation of better ones in the future. It's not uncommon nowadays for one half of a couple to be supported by the other while he or she gets a degree, or completes their training to be a lawyer, accountant, architect or doctor, for example. The 'working' spouse may even stick at a job that he or she dislikes – and may have to work very long hours – while fulfilling the role of sole breadwinner. The pay-off is supposed to be a better lifestyle when the studying partner qualifies. But if the relationship founders before the good times start to roll, then the supporting partner is likely to feel very hard done by.

The types of loss that are suffered during heartbreak are almost as varied as there are people. And as you've been reading these last few pages, I'm sure that some of those that I've mentioned will have struck a chord with you.

I have written about all these different types of loss to help you 'normalise' your own feelings. In grief we can feel pitiful, or pathetic, or weak. So I hope it helps to realise that other men and women have been through similar feelings to your own and that no matter how great any loss may be, people have the capacity to recover from it.

It would be a good idea now for you to write down all the things you've lost as a result of ending the relationship. Then, note down all the things that you've lost because of – or during – the relationship. These lists could prove illuminating reading and might give you a different perspective on your loss.

You see, it's actually not uncommon for our hearts to have been gradually breaking while we were still *within* a relationship – it's just that we've been too focused on holding things together to realise it.

4

Mixed Emotions

At some point during this period of enormous loss, you might well decide that it would have been easier for you if your partner had died, rather than left you. You may even find yourself envying individuals whose relationships have ended in a death. After all, you might think, they were loved to the end of their partner's life, while you've been cruelly abandoned. You may even decide that no widow or widower could begin to understand your humiliation.

In a sense, of course, there are very real similarities between losing someone through death and losing them in life. For a start, both situations are incredibly painful. And people in both categories are likely to go through very complex, mixed emotions, and various stages of grief and mourning.

These emotions and stages are dealt with in greater detail in books on bereavement. But I am also describing them here, albeit quite briefly, because those of you who have been dumped by a partner will experience some of them – and you may feel really frightened by them, or even suspect that you're going mad.

This chapter should help you to see that all these confusing emotions, though horrid, are normal.

Most individuals who have been rejected go through the following stages:

- shock;
- denial;
- panic;
- isolation;
- anger;
- guilt;
- depression.

In fact, it's not uncommon to realise that you've been going through some of these feelings even before the split. Who hasn't felt isolated or angry as a prized relationship lurches towards disaster?

Indeed, on looking back, many adults realise that they'd started grieving for the end of the relationship even before they finally accepted it had to end.

I've already discussed shock at some length in previous chapters, so let's move on to denial.

Denial

Denial tends to happen quite early on in the process of grief, but it can crop up at any time during the period of recovery. In the early days, as I already said, it's common to think that what's happening to you is a nightmare from which you will suddenly waken. You may also comfort yourself with the thought that there's been some terrible mistake. Even though your lover may have walked out on you – perhaps for someone else – you will have moments when you become convinced that the power of your love will prove too strong and that he or she will realise it's impossible to go on without you. You may even fantasise about your ex stumbling through the door, throwing himself or herself at your feet and begging forgiveness.

Of course, sometimes this does happen – particularly after a short-term affair during a long-term marriage. But mostly it doesn't, and it is far better for you if you now convince yourself that you're really on your own – rather than daydream about some unlikely happy ending.

There's another form of denial, which can make sufferers feel that they're going insane. It's a sort of hallucination: they will 'see' their ex on every street corner. And all sorts of images will suddenly seem to strike a stunning resemblance to the beloved. You may look at an advertising hoarding and suddenly 'see' that the model photographed there is the double of your missing loved one. Strangely, if you venture this opinion to anyone else, they will not see the similarity.

You may also become convinced that if you go, right now, to a bar you once went to with your ex, he or she will be there waiting for you.

Amy, a top television producer, took herself off to a country hotel one weekend – a place she and her ex-boyfriend had visited in happier times. She checked in and waited for him to 'tune into her wavelength' and to realise she was there and that they were meant to be together. Of course it didn't happen.

This is the sort of thing that most of us never divulge to our friends or family. So it may come as a bit of a relief to you to realise that it happens to many of us. You see, just as falling in love alters our perspective on life, and removes us – to some extent – from reason and reality, something similar happens when love ends. In truth, we often become quite irrational for a time.

It's very hard to reason with someone who is in the grip of this process. But if you recognise yourself in what I have told you about Amy, then believe me when I say that this kind of behaviour is not uncommon, and not insane – but that it will solve nothing. It's a kind of waking 'wish-dream' and is nothing to do with being in tune with someone else, or about the stars, or about fate – it is just about grief, and is a peculiar manifestation of it.

Panic

Sudden, raw panic that seems to come at you out of nowhere is very frightening. But it's important to realise that it is part of the grief process.

You may suddenly be assailed with panic that you have to face up to a future which is about being single and alone. You may be terrified at the thought of going to parties as a single person, going on holiday, or getting through Christmas. But you are not in a fit state at present to make serious plans about this uncertain future. So, the best thing you can do right now is to deal with these sudden onsets of panic by holding on to something and breathing deeply. In a few moments the panic will pass, and you'll begin to remember that being single has many, many good points. They may not add up to the best of being a couple, but they certainly beat being part of an *unhappy* twosome. And if your relationship had been really happy – well, it wouldn't have fallen apart.

If panic becomes a big problem for you, you might like to contact one of the support groups that can help, such as the National Phobics Society. (Further details can be found in the Directory at the back of the book.)

Isolation

Isolation can be very real – particularly when your love was a forbidden one, or when your relationship cut you off from friends and family. But isolation is one of the things we can actually do something about. It will take some effort, of course, but once you're out of the worst of the shock, you can contact old friends, make new ones, and throw yourself into activities that you always enjoyed and never had time for. And you can also use the Internet and access useful organisations.

It's beneficial if you establish some kind of balance here. Of course, you need time and space to yourself so that you can grieve properly, but you also need to be with people – and if your previous social circle centred almost entirely upon your partner, this is the time when you should establish a new social life.

Anger

Anger can come out of nowhere – and when you least expect it. You might feel hugely angry at yourself for mucking up this special relationship. You might, in your grief, suddenly feel murderously angry towards your parents for not giving you better looks, better social skills, or a more positive example of what a relationship ought to be like. You will probably feel angry with other people who seem to have happy relationships. And you will feel angry with your ex – which is usually a good and healthy sign. In fact, it's much more healthy than sitting at home crying and telling yourself that he or she was perfect and that you'll never get anything as great ever again.

Your partner has hurt you, maybe cheated on you, discarded you, failed you, let you down, and so on – so be angry. Admit to it. Let it out. Get a large cushion and pummel it and cry. You'll feel better afterwards.

But what about anger leading to revenge? This is very tempting – and many people claim to have felt greatly cheered up by getting their own back in some way. There are various apocryphal stories in circulation about women who do things such as pick up their partner's passport, find the section labelled 'Any Distinguishing Marks' and write: 'Very small penis.'

Whether this kind of thing ever really happens, I'm not sure. But something that very definitely *did* happen was the revenge exacted by spurned and humiliated wife, Lady Sarah Graham Moon, against her cheating husband: she raided her husband's wine cellar and delivered two bottles of expensive wine to every doorstep in the village. She cut off one arm of every Savile

Row jacket in his wardrobe and she splashed paint all over his top-of-the-range BMW.

But did it help? It probably *did* help at the time. And of course, Sarah – who now calls herself Sally Moon – achieved a kind of fame as a consequence. That was eleven or so years ago now. And when I interviewed her on a television programme not long afterwards, she told me that while she did not regret her actions, she wouldn't recommend them to others, as they didn't actually help her situation. At that time she was very, very down and very poor, and feeling hugely neglected. She also believed she had no future.

But of course a lot of individuals who had been treated callously by a partner thrilled to her tale – and still do. In fact, I was on a daytime television programme with her recently – and there was much mirth as her exploits were described yet again.

Sally, of course, has moved on. Today she is buoyant and blossoming and she has a lovely man. Indeed, she's a fine advert for the fact that time heals, and also that you can build a new life, and a better one, no matter what your age.

So should you seek revenge? I can't pretend that you wouldn't get some kind of excitement and satisfaction from it. But I can't recommend anything drastic – quite apart from anything else, you might end up being charged for criminal damage.

It's entirely normal to be angry if your lover has left you for another. But, strangely, most individuals reserve their greatest vitriol for their ex's new love, rather than their ex.

I never quite know why that is. Probably it's safer for people to believe that this other, malicious, devious and unscrupulous person led their ex astray. But the truth is that no one can prise someone away from a *perfect* relationship. So, you have to face up to the reality of your situation – which is that your relationship wasn't perfect, that your former partner may well have made the first move in the new relationship and, if not, that he or she was keen to make the second one. I know this sounds harsh, but you need to accept it if you're to get over your current sorrow.

Anger against your departed partner is justifiable and healthy. And you might well manifest it in writing furious letters, bundling their belongings unceremoniously into bin bags and so on. But you must avoid all physical violence or wilful destruction of property. These kinds of acts might even land you in prison and could well seriously damage you or someone else. In the end, this will work against you – not for you.

Stalking, too, is a crazy way to seek revenge or to vent your anger. You may claim that you simply want to get a glimpse of your beloved, or find out what he or she is doing, but this kind of action can become quite addictive and it won't aid your recovery. Furthermore, nowadays, stalking is a criminal offence.

So vent your anger, but be careful how you do it. A session at the gym might help – you can get rid of your aggression and get fitter all at the same time!

One last word on the subject: during your recovery you may find yourself getting totally and unreasonably angry with someone who has nothing to do with your problems. You may have a temper tantrum at work. You may scream at a ticket collector if your train is cancelled. Or you may find yourself on a very short fuse with friends and start telling them home truths which cause offence.

Most people will understand that you're not quite yourself. But you owe it to them to make an apology, and to offer some explanation of why your emotions are so out of control. There is, after all, no reason why you should hurt someone else's feelings just because they happen to get in the way when you're having a bad moment.

Guilt

Guilt is another of the acknowledged stages of grief, and is very common in bereavement, or after a relationship ends. After someone dies, it is quite usual for the spouse to feel that he or she might have done more, or should have been more patient, kind, or loving.

After the breakdown of a relationship, the feelings of guilt are rather different. A person who has been dumped may have little or no guilt – though some rejected individuals may feel guilty that they were 'not enough' for the other person, or that they 'failed' in some way. These feelings are uncomfortable, but they are part of the process of grieving that we all have to go through.

Guilt is much more of a problem, however, for someone who *chooses* to end a relationship. Even if you have been wanting to get out of the relationship for a long time, there is always guilt when you finally do: guilt for having given up on past promises, and guilt at hurting your partner.

This guilt may lead to all sorts of rather over-the-top financial gestures, in a bid to salve the bad feelings. I have known countless people, friends and clients, who, when they finally got out of a long-term relationship, left virtually all their possessions behind in the home they'd shared with their partner – just taking with them a few books, CDs and clothes.

It is certainly right that you should ensure your ex-partner is adequately taken care of financially. But the fact is that no amount of generosity takes the guilt away, so don't go mad! Guilt is normal in these circumstances and it's appropriate that you should feel some. But giving away far more of your worldly goods than is wise, doesn't stop the bad feelings, and may prevent you from getting your financial act together for ages.

One rather more effective way of dealing with guilt is to write a letter to your partner explaining exactly why the relationship has to end. He or she may not be ready to hear or read these things, but you will feel that you have stated your case.

Usually in a break-up, the person being rejected will claim that no explanation was given. Sometimes this is true. But frequently they didn't want to hear one when it was offered. By putting everything down in a letter, you can make sure that your own motives are clear to you and to your ex, and also that there is no misunderstanding about what went wrong and why the relationship is now untenable.

Depression

Depression is often the final stage of grief. But it is frequently difficult to decide where normal misery ends and depression begins.

Obviously, if you have a history of depression, a traumatic event such as the end of a relationship may well spark it off again. But this isn't always the outcome. Sometimes, depression can be caused by being in the *wrong* relationship, and getting out of it can encourage better mental health.

As I've already said, most adults do not plummet into a clinical depression as soon as they break up with their partner, though most men and women *are* excessively miserable. But if your split happened more than ten days ago, and if you are constantly crying, unable to work, or sleep, then you should consider yourself to be depressed. And if you are suicidal too, then as well as seeing your doctor, please tell someone close to you how bad you are feeling, and also call the Samaritans – who are on-call twenty-four hours a day every day.

I would also like to suggest that you get some lay-support for your depression – which you should regard as an illness and not as a sign of weakness. Try the support group Depression Alliance. Also helpful is the health website NetDoctor, which has a whole section on Depression, which is fantastically useful. You'll find further details of both in the Help Yourself Directory at the end of the book.

5

Blame

Blame is a very thorny issue. In the last chapter, I wrote about anger and I mentioned a common urge to blame your ex-partner – or the person who has replaced you in that partner's affections.

But when you're not feeling angry – and especially when you're feeling very sad and miserable – the chances are that you will tend to blame *yourself*. You'll castigate yourself for your lack of sex appeal; you'll condemn yourself because of your inability to sustain relationships; you'll criticise your appearance, or your lack of intellect, or your dullness. And you'll probably decide that you're excessively boring, too quiet, too chatty, or that you're hopeless in every conceivable way.

In other words, you will attach great blame to yourself. This is natural, but not likely to aid your recovery. If a friend of yours were as down on herself as this, you would probably try to persuade her that she wasn't seeing things too clearly – and that she was blaming herself far, far too much. Don't be harder on yourself than you would be on that friend! And try, from now on, to achieve a more balanced view on your part in the downfall of your relationship.

Frankly, 'blame' isn't a very helpful word – although we all use it. It smacks of uncompromisingly rigid condemnation. So instead of looking for who or what to blame, why not try to look for the reasons that forced an end to your relationship?

And before you decide that you can skip this bit – either because you 'know' that all the blame and reasons can be put squarely on your ex or because you believe that all the failure can be attributed to you – let me encourage you to re-think your stance on this.

The truth is that all relationships happen because of the input of two people. And, just as importantly, virtually all relationships *fail* because of the actions of two people. This might be an unpalatable idea, but it's important for you to accept it.

If your husband has walked out after thirty years of marriage and traded you in for a younger model, the chances are that you – or your friends and family – believe he's a rat and that you are a saint. But, if you think about it, the truth may be rather different. Perhaps you let your physical appearance go to pot. Maybe you've put on stones in weight over the years. Perhaps you were bored with sex and always tried to avoid it. Maybe you never interested yourself in his hobbies or his work. Perhaps, once you had children, you put them first. Maybe you nagged your man because he was never tidy in the house, or because he never put up the shelves that you wanted, or because he left the loo seat up all the time. And possibly *you* were pretty bored with the marriage, but would never have left it, because you wouldn't have chosen to face the upheaval and re-thinking that a new single life involves.

None of these things – if they happen to be true – turns you into a sinner rather than a saint; they actually place you some-where between these two extremes, which is where most of us are. They *are*, however, reasons why your husband may have sought attention elsewhere. By saying this, I am not condoning his behaviour, but I am looking at reasons for it. And you should be prepared to acknowledge these reasons.

Let's take another example: what about a situation where a

husband becomes a couch potato? Suppose he likes to stay home watching TV, overeating and drinking, while his wife remains lively and full of fun? Is she to blame if she starts going out clubbing without him, and succumbs to the charms of another bloke? She'll doubtless be portrayed as the guilty party if the marriage falls apart, but she had good reasons for her behaviour. She's not blameless, but neither is her husband.

And what about the freelance journalist who would value his partner's interest and support, but she never reads the articles he writes and only seems to be interested in how much money he can earn? Is he totally to blame if he decides that he'd prefer to be single, rather than misunderstood, unappreciated and lonely within a relationship that is supposed to offer love, support, communication and sharing?

Obviously not. But is his *partner* totally to blame either? No – because she may have her own disappointments within the relationship which have made her hostile to his work.

And what about the situation where a woman goes right off sex and her man eventually finds a new and sexy partner? Well, he may believe that his partner's lack of interest in physical love drove him to leave. But of course, his partner may have gone off sex because his technique in bed was lousy, or because he wasn't sensitive to her needs. Or even because the only time he told her he loved her was when he wanted sex! What I'm saying is that in virtually every break-up, both parties have failed. Not one.

Of course, there are occasional situations where one partner's behaviour is so extremely bad that the spouse has no option but to call 'time' on the relationship. I can think of one woman who realised that her husband was a murderer. She felt she had no option but to lead the police to him – and to end her marriage.

It would be entirely reasonable for a woman who found out that her partner was a child abuser, or a rapist, to terminate the relationship. I knew one man who ended a new and promising romance when he heard his beloved express a harsh opinion of homeless people and asylum seekers. Her views were so different from his own, that he realised their love had no future.

Less dramatically, there are people who love the thrill and the chase of early romance, but who are terrified of any commitment. One could say that they are substantially responsible for the demise of any relationship they're involved in.

And what about relationships ruined by drink or drugs? Clearly partners do leave individuals who are not coping with their addiction. In fact, often they don't leave soon enough. So if you've got yourself out of a romance with someone who had addictive problems, and you believe that you are blameless in that split, then I'm certainly not going to disagree with you.

And then there's violence. I firmly believe that no one – man or woman – should remain in a relationship with a violent partner, no matter how sweet, how contrite, how loving or how much fun that partner might be the rest of the time. If you stay with someone who is violent, you demean yourself – and condone their lack of control.

So – the failure of some relationships is all about the actions or shortcomings of one of the partners. But *most* relationships fall apart because of the actions and behaviour of *both* parties.

It's important to work out the truth of your past relationship and to see it for what it was. But why, you might ask? Why does it help to look at the reasons for the break-up after it's happened? Well, sometimes it can save a relationship at the eleventh hour. Perhaps one partner felt ignored and had an affair but, essentially, the couple had a good marriage, and they had children at home of school age. In this situation they might be able to acknowledge that there had been failures on both sides, and the relationship might then be rescued.

But even if the last thing that is going to happen is that you're going to get back together again, it is useful to understand the reasons why your relationship ended. If you don't get to grips with this reality, you're likely to make the same mistakes all over again with someone else.

As you'll see later in the book, we all bring our own expectations into relationships. We all also have a set of rules that we've evolved to help us deal with life. These expectations and rules – and the way we think – all impact on our relationships, but they're not always helpful. Sometimes patterns need to be broken, and we have to learn to think differently. So by seeing what went wrong – and most particularly why you put up with certain things and what you were intolerant or impatient of – you can appraise your most recent relationship in more realistic terms. You can also make a big difference to your relationships in the future.

6

How Good *Was* Your Relationship?

In the last chapter, I encouraged you to look at the reasons why your relationship failed, and I asked you to consider what *you* may have done wrong, and also what wrong could be attributed to your partner. I expect you're now seeing your past romance in a more realistic way. And by the time you've read *this* chapter, you should have an even greater understanding of it – and how it compares to the sort of relationship that is likely to last.

Often, in our grief, we tell ourselves over and over again that we have lost the love of our life, and that the relationship was perfect. But how great was it really?

I have long believed that many relationships which go *wrong* were never right in the first place! In other words, many people's romances don't offer genuine and authentic love; they don't help them, don't sustain them, aren't any fun, are short on companionship, and absolutely hopeless sexually.

But you're different, aren't you? Your relationship was fine. Or, was it? Seeing it as it really was can help you get over it.

In this chapter I'm going to share with you an inventory I devised some time ago, which consists of twenty-five indicators of a good and compatible relationship. Many individuals would claim to have happy relationships which don't embrace *all* of the points listed below. But if you find that your past romance was pretty deficient in most of them, then you might concede that things weren't that great after all – and that maybe you were allowing yourself to be short-changed.

The Good-Relationship Inventory

In a happy and compatible relationship, adults:

- love each other;
- respect each other;
- are courteous to each other;
- are generally about as physically attractive as one another (this doesn't apply if one of you is very rich and/or powerful!);
- can talk about their feelings together;
- laugh at the same things;
- share similar political views;
- have the same sort of body-clock – i.e. they both like getting up early, or both like staying up late;
- have a similar approach to handling money – or can at least discuss financial matters comfortably;
- have similar sex drives;
- respect each other's religious or moral beliefs;
- are of similar intelligence;
- have broadly similar ages (age difference less than ten years);
- agree on whether or not to have children;
- make an effort to get on with each other's friends and families;
- join in each other's interests – or encourage each other to pursue activities that make them happy, even if they do these alone;
- allow each other time and space to be alone, or to see personal friends;

- take care of each other – especially when one partner is pregnant, ill, tired, or stressed;
- have similar views on how clean and tidy the house should be;
- have similar views on celebrating birthdays/anniversaries;
- enjoy the same sorts of holidays;
- share similar views on issues such as world debt and giving to charity;
- have similar attitudes to health, keeping fit and how much to drink or smoke;
- enjoy the same sort of music, films and TV – or at least make an effort to accommodate differences of opinion;
- believe they are equals in the relationship.

Now, you may say: 'Well, if I'd had all these things in common with my partner, we'd have been clones of each other – not just lovers!' This isn't true, actually. Plenty of good relationships are compatible in all of these ways.

I agree that there are many happy relationships that thrive with less than these twenty-five indicators in place, but when couples share less than fifteen of these, their relationship is generally not viable.

Sometimes, of course, individuals do have most of the points in common – in the early stages. These are relationships which start by being fine, but in which one or other of the partners eventually develops differently – or outgrows it.

If this applies to you, then do accept that you once had a lot going for you both, but also that that time has gone. In addition, try to take on board that there's no reason why you should not find love and compatibility again.

Readers who can see that they were incompatible from the outset – but who hung on in there despite many differences and deficiencies – should acknowledge that they were in a pretty impoverished relationship. If this is your experience, weep for the end of your romance, by all means, but weep for the reality of it. Don't waste your time on falsehoods.

Naturally, you're going to feel very sad – especially if this is the first time you've really accepted that your romantic partnership wasn't up to much. But this acceptance should galvanise you into developing more self-belief and self-regard. It should also encourage you to the view that you will never put up with such a disastrous situation ever again.

Often it's only by facing up to the inadequacies of a previous relationship that we can make sure we get a better one next time.

7

Severing the Connection

Whatever the reality of your past relationship, whether it was good or bad, we come now to a very difficult issue: should you stay in touch or not?

The chances are that you will decide a complete break is far too final, and that you would prefer to have *some* contact. Much will depend upon whether:

- you were the one who ended the relationship;
- the split was a mutual decision;
- you were dumped – and very definitely did *not* want the relationship to end.

Let's look at each scenario in turn.

You Ended the Relationship

You ended the relationship because it was damaging or not going anywhere, or because you've fallen out of love – or have fallen *in* love with another.

If you managed to extricate yourself before you got to the

point of absolutely hating your partner, you may be inclined to soften the blow by suggesting that the two of you remain friends. I have to tell you that, in my view, this is a very bad idea. I'm not saying that you can *never* be friends. Plenty of individuals who were once together do end up as good mates. But it doesn't usually happen right away.

At the time of a break-up, we all need our friends – *other* friends. Furthermore, trying to be good mates with your former lover tends to muddy the waters. If he or she is devastated by the split, any attempt by you to be kind, friendly, or concerned, will be misinterpreted as proof that you either do not know your own mind, or that you are still in love and likely to return.

Is that the message you're trying to give? No? I thought not. But, believe me, this is how the signal will be perceived by your ex.

Of course, if you have children, you're going to have to work out how to continue being joint parents even though you no longer live together – but that is such a big issue that I'm going to devote the whole of the next chapter to it.

So, if your relationship has ended for good, tell it how it is.

Why would you want to stay in contact anyway? You may claim that you were always better friends than lovers – and if that is so, you will probably get to a point one day when you can enjoy each other's friendship all over again. But now is too soon. You may also want to stay in contact so that you won't be identified by all and sundry as a complete louse, and so that people won't hate you! This is understandable. You may have thought very long and hard about this break up. You will almost certainly have very valid reasons for wanting out of the relation-ship – but you may assume that these reasons will not be at all apparent to your friends and relations.

However, after the initial drama and surprise – and even though many people will criticise you for the break-up at the time – you will almost certainly find that a lot of folk have seen the 'hidden' flaws in your relationship and will accept that you did what you had to do. Your mutual friends are unlikely to be stupid. And if your relationship hasn't been great, many of them will have noticed.

It's true that being the person who ends a relationship does not usually endear you to lots of people, but that fact should not keep you in a redundant romance. And it definitely should not encourage you to prolong the parting process.

But what if you change your mind? What if, after a break away from your partner, you wonder if you've made a mistake and you think that having your ex-partner as a friend will clarify the situation for you? Well, people do change their mind all the time.

Adults who have affairs, for example, sometimes leave the marital nest and then find the new relationship doesn't work out and they want to scuttle back to the old one.

Or sometimes a person leaves the old relationship ready to have a new, brilliant single life, but finds that the new life fails to live up to expectations. Such an individual may be further confused by discovering that his or her ex-partner is blossoming, has lost a stone in weight, looks ten years younger, and is out clubbing every night.

Is it fair and legitimate in these situations to try to forge a friendship with the ex while trying to sort out your emotions? I don't think so. If you genuinely want to get back together again, you should explain your uncertainty and beg for a second chance to be a loving and equal partner. If your ex then takes you back it should be because he or she still loves you and wants you as a partner – and is prepared to work at a loving relationship with you.

I'm not saying, by the way, that you should necessarily seek, or expect, to be reinstated immediately and fully back into a cohabiting and sexual relationship. Not at all. I believe you should both take things very slowly. But be honest in your wants and hopes and needs. And remember that being a partner is not the same thing at all as being friends.

A Split by Mutual Decision

If a split is genuinely mutual, I do believe that friendship can be salvaged quite quickly – but not immediately. In fact, *staying* friends – without a break of any kind – in the early stages of a relationship break-up can be counterproductive, and can stop you finding new romance.

If, for example, you both believe that your relationship is over – perhaps you don't fancy each other any more, or else you each want different things from the relationship – but find that being together has become such a cosy habit that you continue to hang out together, then neither of you is likely to find a new love. You need to have a break from each other in order to establish new contacts and new habits.

Such couples often started a relationship when they were both at school or university. They got on well, they saw each other through their finals, they had loads of mutual friends, and they may well have lived with each other in a flat-share situation before they became an exclusive item.

There's nothing wrong with this sort of union. In fact, I count as friends several couples who fall into this category, and who are happily still together in their fifties. But sometimes, such a twosome come to realise that their relationship is all about friendship rather than love – and that if they're to find real romance and have children, they need to do it with other people.

This can be very sad, even if it's the right decision. In such a situation it's a good idea if both parties lean on other friends individually for a time and branch out and do new things: go travelling, change jobs, or move to another part of the country. Anything, in fact, that will reinforce their decision that it's right to move on, and to find the kind of love that will lead to a grown-up, sexual and hopefully permanent relationship.

As anyone who's tried to give up smoking knows, breaking a habit is hard. And this habit – your former relationship – still has much to commend it. So it will be difficult to walk away from it, if you don't both give yourselves time and space to start building your new lives. A good action plan would be to agree not to contact each other for three months.

There are two possible pitfalls to this kind of planned, mutually agreed split: the first is if you have children together. A clean split in such cases, with no contact, is not possible. I have to put my cards on the table here and say that if adults have a young family, I honestly believe that they should make every effort to stay together for as long as is feasible, so as to give their kids the best security possible. And in the kind of relationship I've been describing – well, things usually aren't so bad that they can't be endured for a few more years at least. But I'll return to the subject of kids in the next chapter.

The second pitfall is that one or other of you – in your bid to exercise your freedom – may get into another relationship quite quickly. Unfortunately, the mood between the two of you may darken quite dramatically as a result. Where before you were both talking happily of making new and separate lives, marrying, having children and getting out into the world and having brave new adventures, suddenly the one who *hasn't* so far hooked up with a new love can become deeply hurt, and sometimes vitriolic.

This can be a big shock to both parties. Where there was sadness but no heartbreak, this new circumstance can generate a massive amount of pain, and also endanger the friendship you were both so keen to preserve.

Obviously, no one should emerge from a relationship feeling prohibited from having a new sexual and romantic partner. But the decent thing is to keep quiet about it for a while – and this is much easier if you have agreed not to stay in close contact for quite a while.

The truth is that friendship is not really possible or desirable while you make the break, so you should forget the whole idea of being friends until the dust has settled.

The Split Has Been Forced Upon You

If you've been dumped, and if you still believe that you truly love this person who's dumping you, you will almost certainly grab any tiny crumb of comfort that your partner offers you.

So if she says: 'I really hope that we can stay friends...' you'll feel such relief at the promise of *some* contact with your loved one, that you won't stop for a moment to consider whether or not this is good for you.

Or if he says: 'I'd like to pop round once a week and check that you're OK', you'll probably clutch at him and insist he makes a date for his first visit there and then. Don't be ashamed – we've all done it!

But – and this is the important thing – you don't need this person to be your friend. You *have* friends. If you haven't, it's high time you got out there and made some.

You need a loving partner. That's what you really want – and you probably want this person whom you still love to fulfil that role.

It's true that you may have been friends for a long time, but you have also been lovers, and that's changed everything. He or she is withdrawing from that role – and to get over this, you both need to give up all contact, for now. Hanging on to some small offer of friendship will not benefit you. Trust me. You will interpret every small kindness as meaning that he or she still loves you. You will focus and depend on your meetings. This will keep you so firmly in the past – mentally – that you will not accept that your relationship is over, neither will you start grieving properly, or begin to rebuild your life. I know this, because I see it in my clients all the time. I also know it from painful, personal experience.

I once let a hopeless romance of mine drag on for almost three years, hoping and praying that it was going to improve and I lapped up every tiniest bit of attention he proffered – but I became seriously depressed in the process. I simply would not accept that a relationship which had promised so much was going no further.

I can see now that my ex-boyfriend had enormous problems about committing to a long-term relationship, but that he felt better about hurting me if he rang me up constantly, and regularly took me out for lunch. He didn't want me to hate him after what we had meant to each other. And we had been deeply in love.

Unfortunately, his phone calls and invitations became my lifeline. I let myself believe that so long as we kept in contact there was a chance he would want to be with me. I suppose the fact that he was kind and still appeared to care was the only thing that mattered to me at that time. But it didn't help me. It just caused prolonged grief.

So he was at fault, although I like to believe that he acted from the purest of motives. And I was at fault, because I refused to accept the very clear signals that the relationship could not continue.

So, take it from a veteran of a protracted split that was hugely damaging, that a clean break is the toughest thing you'll ever have to go through. But you'll emerge from it more quickly in the long run – and with much more of your self-respect and self-esteem intact.

Remember that trying to stay friends with someone through the trauma of broken romance is a mug's game. It might make your previous partner feel better about dumping you – but it sure as hell won't help you one jot.

Of course, many readers of this book will have been in a situation where their partners claimed to be confused about the relationship, so rather than ending it, they asked to stay friends, but also begged for some time and space to sort themselves out.

I think most of the individuals who act in this way *are* actually sure that they want to end it, but want to hedge their bets, in case they feel lonely. They may also believe that by breaking up in stages, the process will be less traumatic and painful all round.

This is rarely so. A friend of mine willingly gave her man the time and space to sort his head out – which he decided to do in the Bahamas. She felt very bitter when she later discovered that he had taken a much younger woman to share his time and space with him.

Then there are those who claim to be going through a mid-life crisis, and who say that they need to 'live on their own for a bit', but who have also already made up their minds to start new lives. Such individuals frequently keep up this pretence for years – often in a bid to avoid a costly divorce.

I think this is a particularly unkind way to end a relationship. It plays on the rejected partner's vulnerability and gives her (and it nearly always is a 'her') hope that her man will return. He may very well set up home – either alone or with someone else – but he will return to the family nest for mother-in-law's birthday, Christmas, their children's graduation days, her birthday, or Sunday lunch. You name it, he's there. In fact, he now has what he's probably always wanted – a bit of family life, but the life of a single man too.

Is this what's happening to you? If so, how do you feel about it now that you see it in black and white? Don't you think you're being taken for a ride? Don't you feel that you're travelling through a long tunnel of pain that never ends?

Contact with someone who no longer wants to play a leading role in your life is usually damaging. As I said earlier, eventually you may be able to be civilised to each other, and perhaps you'll even become friends again. But while your heart is broken, the offer of friendship and contact is unhelpful.

Severing all connection with your ex may feel like the worst form of torture – but if a relationship has to end, this is the best way to do it.

8

Especially for Parents

Getting over a broken heart is a painful process for anyone – but it's especially difficult and complicated if you have children.

In Chapter Seven, I suggested that you should avoid all contact with your past lover. You may be wondering how, as a parent, this is remotely possible. It may not be – especially in the early stages of your split. So, although I believe that the sooner you can reach a point where you *don't* have to see your ex the better, first you're going to have to properly sort out all sorts of practical and emotional issues concerning your children. And unless one of you is going to give up all idea of being a mum or dad to your offspring – not something that I could ever recommend – then you're going to need to find some method of joint-parenting.

This is, of course, going to involve contact between you both. You might think that it would be better for your kids if that contact could be friendly: if, indeed, the two of you could remain friends, now and for ever.

In an ideal world, this would be marvellous. But just because you're a parent, it doesn't follow that you'll be able to handle being with your ex. One of you, at least, is likely to be feeling hugely angry, or depressed, or abandoned – and will want to cling on to any possible friendship between you in the hope that it will rekindle the relationship. For all the reasons set out in the previous chapter, this is a bad idea.

So, how can you proceed in order to give yourself the best chance of recovery from the split, but in such a way that you can provide as much continuity of care and security for your family as possible?

Basically, you need to sort out plausible and practical ways in which you can both continue to parent your kids lovingly and effectively, while also taking care of your own best interests. To do this, I'd like to encourage you to tap into all the resources that are now at your disposal. (Further details of everything I mention in this chapter can be found in the Directory at the back of this book.)

Books, Support Groups, Lawyers and Mediation

There are, for example, a number of excellent books on divorce and separation, such as: *Find Your Way Through Divorce* by Jill Curtis, and *Moving On: Breaking Up Without Breaking Down* by Suzie Hayman.

There are websites, such as On Divorce and the National Association for the Divorced and Separated.

There are legal organisations such as the Solicitors' Family Law Association, whose aim is to get their clients through the whole process of separation or divorce without increasing hostility on both sides. (And I can assure you that not all lawyers fall into this category.)

There are associations, such as Gingerbread and the National Council for One-Parent Families – to help you in your new role as a single, or part-time parent.

And, perhaps most importantly of all, there are mediation agencies such as The UK College of Family Mediators,

Family Mediation Scotland and National Family Mediation. Mediation is a process by which you can jointly agree a fair set of arrangements for your future lives. This is an excellent process for any separating or divorcing couple to go through, but in my view it is especially desirable to do it if you have children – even though, currently, there is no legal requirement for you to do so. Frequently, people who go through mediation actually save money in legal costs. More vitally, by being able to talk together in the presence of an impartial mediator, they can sort out the future of their children in a civilised and appropriate way.

If you opt for mediation, you will need to attend meetings together, which may be difficult for both of you – but the conciliators are experienced in handling vulnerable, angry, in-transigent, depressed individuals who are traumatised by the emotional maelstrom of a broken relationship. By putting your future in the care of these professionals, you'll be able to sort out how your children are going to be brought up from now on, and by whom. Once this is finalised, you can get on with going through your stages of grief and rebuilding your life.

The Mistakes Parents Often Make

One reason for having mediation – or even family or relation-ship therapy – is that these processes help you to understand your feelings and your motives.

But as you may choose *not* to get any help of this kind, in this section I'm going to try to help you avoid some common mistakes that parents make when they have no one to help them.

It is, for example, quite usual for parents who are hurting because of the demise of a relationship to 'use' their children as friends, counsellors, or simply a shoulder to cry on. They also try – albeit in many cases at a subconscious level – to get the children on their side.

All this is a terrible mistake. Although it's understandable that you should want the kids to know your side of the story, and though you may think it's perfectly reasonable that when you're feeling very sad you should enlist their sympathy, in fact, children should not be used in this way. If you need to cry on someone's shoulder, find a grown-up – don't use your kids.

If you want to explain why you're getting out of the relationship, or why your ex-partner is such a louse, explain to your vicar, your doctor, your siblings, your parents, or your friends. *Don't* unload all this stuff on your children.

Never forget that half of the genes in your child's body come from your ex. Parents who assume that a child is totally on their side, or who believe that a child is happy to never see the other parent, tend to store up real trouble for themselves for later on.

I know it's difficult, but if your children are going to have the best chance of getting over this upheaval, you and your co-parent should present a loving, joint front for your kids whenever and wherever possible. This means telling them that though you both love them very much, the two of you no longer love each other.

You also need to impress upon them that the split is not their fault. Frequently, kids think that if they'd been better behaved and hadn't added to the stress in the home, that Mum and Dad would have been able to stay together. You need to disabuse them of this notion. Very often, parents are in such turmoil and pain that they forget to ask their children what they're feeling – and so these anxieties can go unchallenged and can lead to all sorts of strains and misery.

You also need to emphasise that you are going to care for them jointly, as far as that is possible, and that you're going to make any big decisions about their future *together*. Also explain that you're going to try to make things as normal as they can be, as *soon* as they can be.

A common mistake to make – and it's a particular

temptation for the live-in parent – is to make it very difficult for your ex to see the children. It's understandable that this parent – usually the mother – may be feeling very hurt and rejected, but keeping your kids from your ex is *not* the way to deal with those feelings.

I've heard endless tales – usually from dads – saying that they drove a hundred miles on a Sunday to see their children and their ex refused to let the children come out, or claimed they didn't want to see their father, or that they had colds.

I can only urge you to try not to resort to such behaviour yourself, no matter how broken-hearted or angry you might feel. Your children will almost certainly come to resent your tactics – and you may end up being seen as a moral blackmailer or manipulator.

I knew a very intelligent woman who took her rejection by her husband really badly, and who made it as difficult as possible for her daughter Milly to see her dad.

'He was never around for Milly anyhow,' she told me. 'Not even when he lived with us, so Milly doesn't miss him at all. And she's so good. When I'm miserable at night she mops up my tears and tells me that she never wants to see her daddy again as long as she lives. She's such a comfort to me.'

This woman, despite her intelligence, was making every mistake in the book. And now that Milly is in her late teens, what has happened? She blames her mum for making her lose contact with her dad. She has no time for her maternal relatives, and she has gone out of her way to seek male company and approval from a variety of unsuitable men – and has ended up pregnant before leaving school.

Of course, if you've emerged from a relationship that was violent, or if your ex-partner always treated you with contempt, or had a string of affairs before finally leaving, then you could certainly be forgiven for not portraying him as a saint! But even so, do try to keep your criticism to a minimum in front of your kids. They need to make up their own minds about your ex, and they also need to accommodate the fact that they are that parent's flesh and blood – just as they are also yours.

Teaching a child to dislike a parent can have serious consequences for that youngster – well into adult life. Many of the men and women I see in my practice have very poor self-esteem. And often this lack of esteem seems to have arisen because these people were taught to ignore – or even to hate – a missing parent. By association, they began to hate themselves, or at least to feel uneasy with any similarities they could see between themselves and their 'bad' parents.

The other day I had a letter from a guy called Martin, who wanted to tell me how he had grown up in a very female-dominated household: a household where men were derided, and where he was taught that men were not to be trusted. In fact, it was so anti-male that he felt quite ashamed of his gender.

Martin's father had escaped from Czechoslovakia during their troubled times in the late sixties. He had come to Scotland and married Martin's mother. Martin arrived on the scene shortly afterwards – and a few years after that, his parents' marriage failed.

Martin told me that he could remember his mother and maternal grandmother laughing at his dad's poor command of English and mocking him because he could only get a menial job.

Eventually, Martin's father disappeared with a much kinder woman. Privately, Martin could not find it in his heart to blame his father. But his mum made it plain to him that she would consider it very disloyal if he ever saw his dad again.

During the next few years as he grew up, Martin's mother and grandmother continued to reinforce his early ideas that being male was a second-rate category and that people from Eastern Europe were pretty hopeless – and certainly different and odd. He is now convinced that his poor self-esteem stems from that time.

His early adult life was very miserable. He found it difficult to carve out a career and to make relationships. Luckily, Martin could see for himself that he needed help and he got some therapy which helped him a lot.

Some years later, he has come to understand that he was given a very one-sided view of half of his genes! He has now re-established contact with his father, and he has been to Prague several times to meet relatives and to explore his European side.

He has felt welcomed by his father's family and he can see how like them he is. Now he feels as if he has come to terms with himself and he is a much happier person. He feels complete and valid. But it has taken him years of hard work to get to this point.

You may think that Martin's case is extreme. But I can tell you that stories like his are not that unusual. So, even in the midst of your own horror and misery, think hard before you overly criticise your ex in front of your children, or keep them from seeing him or her. You never know what trouble this may cause later on.

Another common mistake is for parents to get cross with each other in front of their children. This usually happens when the parent who has the kids at weekends turns up to collect them. To avoid this happening, and, as I've already suggested, to keep your contact with your ex down to the minimum, it can be beneficial to get your ex to pick up the children from a neutral environment, rather than the family home. Maybe your parents would agree that your former spouse can collect the kids from *their* house – if they live near enough to you. Or perhaps a friend can drop them off to your ex and pick them up after the visit.

This kind of arrangement may not be all that easy to manage, but I cannot emphasise enough how awful it is for children to witness hostility between their parents. And I stress, yet again, how difficult it is for the adults to get over the loss of the relationship if they continue to see each other all the time. It's pretty much like ripping a plaster off a wound before it's properly healed – and starting the bleeding all over again.

Up until now, I've mostly talked about the parent who has the children living with him or her. So let's turn to other situations where mistakes are made. These days, there are some couples who decide to live so close to each other after their split that they can genuinely share the children between them. They tell me that they each have the child for half the week and that this works well.

These couples are in a tiny minority, however. And I'm not sure myself, especially as the children get older, that this scenario *does* work that well – particularly not from the kids' point of view, as they seem to be constantly on the move.

In most cases, one parent has the children all through the week while the other gets to see them at weekends and in the school holidays. Many of the weekend-only parents are people who have chosen to leave because they've found a new partner. They may indeed be fabulously in love with that partner, but even so, it's likely that such individuals feel enormous guilt and can feel truly heartbroken about what they've done to their kids and how little they are now able to see them. It's easy in these circumstances to over-compensate the children by making the weekends one long round of fun and extravagance. This is a common mistake.

Frankly, not only does such behaviour seriously upset your ex partner, but it also distorts your relationship with your kids. If you turn every day into an experience to rival Christmas, you'll never do anything normal.

And it's *normal* things that your kid will crave. Of course, if you're stupid enough to shower your offspring with luxury toys and games, they're hardly going to turn them down! But what they want most – and what they'll be missing most – is ordinary contact with you. They'll want to be able to talk to you – and that's not easy if you're always in a cinema, or amusement arcade, or on a fairground ride.

You may have had very good reason for splitting up from your children's other parent. You may, in fact, not be at all heartbroken about that split – perhaps because it was long overdue. But you may well find yourself really cut up because you don't see enough of your kids. This is understandable. But it won't help you or them if you spoil them.

Kids often like doing very basic things, such as coming to your new home – even if it's only a temporary bedsit – and having you cook sausages and beans for them which you can eat while watching the telly. Trying to create expensive surprises every week will wear you and your children out – and make a major dent in your pocket just when it's likely that your finances are far from rosy.

And what if you have a new partner – someone you love? Well, if you have, you'll probably long for this special person to meet your family. And you'll probably secretly believe that they will immediately adore each other. But how wrong you might be! Your children will have endured enormous upheaval as a result of your original relationship breaking up: upheaval that has been forced on them and is definitely not of their choosing. It's unlikely, therefore, that they'll feel well disposed to the person they think has caused all the trouble.

So making them meet your new love before they're ready is a bad mistake. In my view, you need at least six months of taking your kids out on your own and being there for them before you even suggest introducing them to your new partner.

And even when your kids and your partner have met, please don't assume that you can all spend the weekends together in future. Your children have no history with this new person of yours. They need to see you alone so that they can discuss things that matter to them, and have some private time with you.

All this is very difficult to arrange during a period which is stressful and often financially worrying and emotionally chaotic. But unless you want to put up insurmountable barriers between you and your children, you really need to find good, quality time for them right now. If you don't, then you may suffer a very lengthy heartbreak that may never heal.

Some parents – and these are almost invariably dads – find themselves living apart from their children even if they were the parent who was dumped. They really do have a very tough emotional mountain to climb. Not only are they often heart-broken by the loss of the partner they loved, but also they are usually distraught at having to leave the family home and, as a result, having only limited contact with their kids. It can seem monumentally unfair – and it's easy to see why such people often feel very bitter indeed.

If this is your experience, whatever you think of your ex-partner, the law, and the injustices of life, please remember – as I've already said – that your children are composed of her genes as well as yours. So try not to make the mistake of showing your offspring how angry you feel. If you do, you will almost certainly come to regret it.

Nowadays, there are plenty of other men in the same boat – you'll almost certainly know some. Lean on them. There are also organisations where you can meet fathers in a similar situation – such as Families Need Fathers – and where you can get support from people who understand exactly what you're going through.

Very sadly, about 50 per cent of men who split from their children's mother drift away out of those children's lives within two years. As we've already seen, this may well be because the mother makes life so very problematic for the father to see the children that he finally decides it will be less trauma all round if he bows out of the picture. But this can be heartbreaking – and it's one of the worst mistakes you can make.

If you disappear from your child's life, it's unlikely that your ex will speak kindly of you. She may even hide presents or letters that you send, so that your poor youngsters are forced to conclude that you simply couldn't be bothered to stay in touch – and that you never really loved them.

There's a great deal of heartbreak when a family splits up, but don't make it worse by giving up on your kids – no matter how difficult things get. They need you.

Tough though it very definitely is, you have to be very adult in this situation, and – no matter how heartbroken you are – you must put your kids first. Once they're OK, then you can focus on yourself.

9

Affairs

This is a chapter for anyone who is heartbroken over an affair – their own or someone else's.

Affairs almost always cause trouble – for someone. They may start as a little bit of fun when people are lonely or bored, or simply looking for a little bit of excitement – and the participants may claim at that stage that they 'can handle it'. But most of these liaisons end up by causing heartache all round.

The word 'affair' covers everything from the briefest of sexual dalliances, to real love matches that endure for decades. Personally, however, I don't choose to dignify a one-night stand by using the word 'affair'. A one-night stand very often happens when people are drunk. Many of them occur when people who would normally be at home find themselves thrown together overnight, in unusual circumstances. Situations such as summer schools, sales conventions and business conferences are all fertile breeding grounds for this kind of hanky-panky.

Now I actually believe that it is possible for someone to have a good relationship at home, but still somehow find him or herself having a one-night stand – because of loneliness or drunkenness, or both. On the whole, one-night stands are pretty dire. Occasionally, I suppose, adults feel better for having had some relief from sexual tension. But much more often, they're worried about what people will think, whether their partners will get to hear about it, and whether or not they might have picked up a disease or got pregnant.

A real affair – unlike a one-off one-night stand – is very *unlikely* to happen when a long-term relationship is in good shape. Basically, when people are happy with each other they don't even *notice* someone else putting out enticing signals! This is an important point – especially for anyone whose partner or ex-partner has had an affair.

As I discussed in Chapter Six, people in perfect relationships rarely stray. So, if you're going to recover from your partner's affair – and maybe even take him or her back – you're going to have to face the unpalatable truth that things couldn't have been entirely OK at home before the affair began. This means that even if you think your partner's been an absolute bastard to betray you in this way, a full reconciliation is unlikely unless you can see that there were problems within your relationship prior to the affair.

Nowadays, affairs are very common. Traditionally, it was married men who had them – usually with younger, single women. But now that we women have efficient contraception, and the freedom that comes from having a career and income, affairs are just as likely to involve married or cohabiting females.

Unfortunately, because of the secret nature of most affairs, the ending of them can be a very solitary business. Even if you *do* confide in a friend about it, you may well be told that: 'Well you knew there was no future in it, didn't you?' Or: 'Everyone knew you were playing with fire – and now you've got burnt.' Or, perhaps worst of all, 'Well, you weren't the first and you won't be the last.'

To discover that this person you loved has had a string of illicit liaisons is extraordinarily painful – even long after your affair has ended. Very many affairs evolve in the workplace. So when they end, it's commonplace for people's jobs to become quite untenable. Having to see your ex-lover daily when you are struggling to get over him or her is not a good idea – as we have already seen in Chapter Seven. But, worse than this, is that when one of the lovers is senior to the other, the firm may very well protect the senior person at the expense of the junior employee.

For example, secretaries get moved to another department while bosses remain in their own comfortable swivel chairs. Sometimes, life at work can be made so intolerable for one participant of a recently ended affair, that the only sane course of action is for that person to leave.

You may be reading this book having lost not only your love, but also your livelihood. Of course, you can try to fight what is happening to you – either through your Human Resources Department, or with help from your trade union if you belong to one – but, in practice, most people don't. It takes a hell of a lot of courage at a time when you are at your most sad and vulnerable.

It's hurtful enough if you get dumped from a relatively short-term affair – especially if it involves your job too – but being rejected after having loved someone secretly for years is a truly devastating experience for many people.

Nowadays, it isn't just women who get hurt in this way.

Shaun is a young freelance journalist. He met Anthea – fifteen years his senior – when he showed her how to use the 'Pec Deck' at the gym.

Afterwards, in the juice bar, she bought him a drink and they got chatting. The attraction was immediate and their affair began soon afterwards. Shaun had recently been dumped by his girlfriend and was more than ready for some female appreciation. Anthea was married to a highly success-ful businessman who was the managing director of a chain of department stores.

Anthea claimed to be unhappy in her marriage. Her children were away at university and, she said, her husband was too busy to pay her any attention. He wasn't, she said, interested in the theatre, or music, or any of the things that she felt made life worth living. She told Shaun that *he* was everything that her husband was not.

As for Shaun, he was besotted. Anthea was older and she certainly knew her way round the human body. She was confident in bed and eager for lots of sex. He believed she was the woman he'd waited for all his life – and after they'd been seeing each other for over a year, he asked her to leave her marriage.

She kept promising that she'd think about it – and that she'd talk to her husband about what was happening. But she never did. Eventually, Shaun gave her an ultimatum – 'him or me' – and she disappeared from his life. She wrote to him saying that she wasn't prepared to divorce, because she didn't want to cause upheaval for her kids.

Afterwards, Shaun wished that he'd simply gone on as they were rather than lose her. But he knew that they'd got to the stage where the relationship, as it was, simply wasn't enough for him.

Unfortunately, no one in his life knew about Anthea – so losing her left an enormous void which he couldn't discuss with anyone.

He also started to question how much he had actually meant to her. And he tormented himself with thoughts that she preferred her comfortable lifestyle to sharing his rather ramshackle existence.

He saw her occasionally, by chance, but she never acknowledged him again, and he got the feeling that her life had been untroubled by the affair and that – as far as she was concerned – it was as if he'd never been part of it. He found this a very bitter and agonising experience – and a very lonely one.

Some months later, when he came to my consulting room, he said: 'I hope this doesn't sound petty, but what I really want to know is whether I was just a distraction for her, or whether she really loved me? But *she* won't tell me and I have no one else to ask. And now I feel as though I've drowned, and the waters have closed over my head. It's as if our love didn't bother her in any sense at all. I've never felt more bereft in my life.'

It took Shaun a long time to recover and to find someone new to love and trust.

Kate's experience was just as painful: she had been the long-term lover of a college lecturer. Their affair had begun when she was a student and he was her tutor. He claimed to have fallen incandescently in love with her, but insisted that he couldn't leave his wife and children.

Kate was so in love that she put up with never seeing him on her birthday, or at Christmas, or during the holidays, and also never quite knowing if he would turn up when he said he would.

She also put up with his extreme moodiness. He could become very depressed – seemingly for no reason – and when that happened, he would avoid her. Or, if he *did* see her, he would come round for sex in the usual way, but be remote and unloving.

During those moody spells she was always fearful that he had tired of her. She used to feel panic-stricken, because she loved him so much. But he always recovered, and then he thanked her for sticking by him – and his gratitude always renewed the bond between them.

As his children grew older, he promised her that one day he would leave his wife. But time went on. His children went off to university. And, with a shock, Kate realised that her affair had been going on for seventeen years: years when very few people knew about her love life. Years when she might have expected to get married. Years when she would certainly have liked to have started her own family.

She consoled herself with the thought that their love was special, and that soon all would be well.

Well, eventually, her lover *did* leave his wife. But he didn't leave his wife for Kate. He left for a fellow lecturer.

Kate's situation is not unusual, unfortunately. So, if *you're* in an affair that never goes anywhere, and you are feeling heart-broken but are still sticking with it, please take on board the fact that long-term affairs rarely end in marriage. Time and time again, they provide love and support for a married, or cohabiting, person who either never leaves home, or who – in the end – leaves for someone else entirely.

If an individual is going to break up a marriage or cohabiting relationship for his or her new love, it generally happens in the first few months of the affair, not after years and years. I believe that getting over the end of an affair is a particularly awful form of heartache – and people in this situation tend to be very hard on themselves.

If you're trying to handle the end of an affair, you may well harangue yourself for your stupidity in hanging on to something that – you now see – was never going to go anywhere. You may feel enormous guilt for hurting your lover's spouse. You may feel bitterness at the way you've been treated. You may think that nothing ever works out for you – and therefore that you must be a horrible or worthless person.

In Part Two of this book, we'll be looking at how you can rethink these kinds of thoughts and feelings – and get over them. But for now, the most important step you can take is to lavish care on yourself and to get some support from someone you can trust. And if you really can't face talking to any of your friends or family, there would be a case for going and talking to a Relationship Counsellor.

Finally, please remember that just because the world knew nothing of your love, it doesn't mean that it never happened, or that it wasn't important. Your love for this other person was true and valid. And with your capacity for loving, you can definitely love again.

10

Good and Bad Behaviour

This last chapter in the 'Accepting it' section of the book is all about the good things you can do for yourself as you begin to emerge from your heartbreak. It's also about the sort of behaviour that is best avoided.

Practicalities

To some extent, you may already have had to make various changes in your life because of your heartbreaking situation. Perhaps you've had to leave your house or flat, or maybe you're still in the family home, but fear that in order to make ends meet you're going to have to sell it. Perhaps you're in the process of 'buying out' your partner so that you can stay in the flat you shared.

Such practical changes are often forced upon us when our relationship folds. And, just as a widow may not feel too bad while she is arranging her husband's funeral in the days immediately following his death, you may have been so busy dealing with these practicalities that you've not had too many empty moments to grieve for your past.

But when things are sorted, you can feel very anti-climatic and lacking in energy – and it may suddenly hit you just how different your life is going to be from now on. So try to prepare yourself for these feelings, and if they happen, do remind yourself that they are normal.

But what of other changes? Are they a good thing right now? In a bid to feel better, individuals have been known to make extraordinary lifestyle alterations at this time. A woman I know – whose make-up and nails were always perfect, who had endless sets of matching lingerie, and whose idea of roughing it was to go to a three-star rather than a five-star hotel – suddenly decided to set off backpacking round the world when her man left her.

None of her friends could believe it – and cheerfully forecast that she'd come home before the month was out. She proved them wrong. She travelled through the Far East not only handling the money, the language barrier, and the insects – but also managing to survive with only two pairs of knickers! When she finally returned to the UK she was a very different person. She had triumphed.

It's quite common nowadays for people to decide that the end of a relationship is a great time to go travelling. But, despite the story I've just told you, my advice would be to wait a few months before you do it. Certainly, some people do derive great personal satisfaction from doing something brave and entirely different – and they are anxious to get going right away. But for everyone who copes, there are plenty who don't. The truth is that you won't leave your heartache behind when you quit these shores. It will travel with you. For this reason, I believe that most adults feel better in the early months if they surround themselves with all the support that normality can offer – usual job, usual friends, usual family, usual location and so on.

But I do think that if you've always planned to travel, you can cheer yourself up enormously by making detailed plans to get away after three to six months of being alone.

Many hurt people also consider holidays. Again, do be aware that your sadness may seem worse if you've got plenty of time to sit around in the sun and think about it. And don't make the mistake of going somewhere that used to mean something special to the two of you.

There are companies who organise travel for single people, and I would strongly urge you to book with one of them if you do decide that you want to get away. But it would be wise to leave it for a month or so.

One excellent break you can take at any time is to a health farm. Here you can eat both well and wisely. You can have treatments, and relax. And because no one is rushing off at the end of the day, you'll almost certainly find someone to talk to.

Health farms seem to be favourite places for folk to go when their relationships are in trouble, or have just ended – so you nearly always find plenty of other individuals with whom you can empathise and share your troubles.

Do make sure to get a massage while you're there. When we feel low and vulnerable we tend to find it hard to indulge ourselves. But, as you probably know by now, I'm very keen that you should do just that.

Massage is an especially good thing to have when you're miserable. It can be very heartening to have someone else's hands all over your body. Touch is important to lonely or sad people. And of course a skilled operator will ease away all those knots of tension that have accumulated during these very sorrowful times.

So a short break at a health farm can be a very good idea, but on balance, it's probably better to delay any other decision on getting away from home.

What about moving house? Apart from a house move that is forced upon you, I would urge caution. Maybe you've always hankered after a completely different life. You might – while 'strap-hanging' on the London underground – suddenly decide that it would be great to live in the depths of Devon. Or, if you're Irish but living in England, you may feel the call of your roots and get a real urge to go back to 'where you belong'.

I'm all for people taking life by the scruff of the neck, but again I urge caution. Most people who are in the aftermath of a break-up are not thinking straight. By all means get a lot of information about what you'd like to do and start planning for it. But don't actually implement your plans for at least three months.

Francesca had always wanted a dog, but had never owned one. On the very day her husband left her, she went to a nearby kennels and bought herself a Labrador puppy. There were, of course, bonuses to her purchase. Here was a little fluffy bundle for her to love, and which would love her unconditionally in return.

But Francesca had lots of friends scattered throughout the UK who wanted to help her. As soon as they heard of her troubles, they were all keen to invite her to stay – and she quickly realised that not everyone would welcome her untrained puppy.

Furthermore, she hadn't realised what havoc a young dog can create during a working day while its owner is out at work. And when she was feeling really miserable, the discovery of another pool of puppy-pee in a corner, or the badly chewed corner of an antique table, were not welcome diversions – in fact, they made her cry.

In time, Francesca *did* manage to house-train her Labrador, and she also found a retired neighbour who was only too pleased to walk the puppy during the day when she had to work. But she was forced to admit that buying a dog – without thinking through all the consequences – wasn't the brightest thing she could have done when she was already under huge stress.

So, to sum up – yes, you will want to make changes, and there's nothing wrong with that. But don't make very big ones until you've been on your own for a while and are sure about them.

New Projects

As you begin to adjust to being single again, you will realise that you've got quite a lot of time on your hands. Time that otherwise you would have spent with your partner.

At first you won't be in much of a mood to use this time productively, but the day will come when you have more energy for new projects. Plenty of newly single people, for example, decide to join a gym to lose weight and to enhance their social lives. This is generally a good plan.

To make it work for you, I suggest you shop around first. Don't join the first gym you see. Check a few out. And if you want to enjoy it, then join the best one you can afford – the one with plenty of space, good equipment, trained supervisors, a swimming pool, café on site and, possibly, with a beauty or hairdressing salon attached. A crèche is another great facility if you have kids.

However, don't take on too much exercise too soon. At my gym, I often see new people turn up – often extremely unfit people at that – and right from the first day they insist on doing twenty minutes on the treadmill, sweating over huge weights and rowing for half an hour. Not surprisingly, their enthusiasm for fitness quickly fades!

If you give yourself too strenuous a schedule, then the day when you don't feel like going – because it's all far too much effort – will come very quickly.

So, start small: do four minutes on the rowing machine, three minutes on the treadmill. Do lots of stretching, some not-too-heavy weights, and restrict yourself to maybe fifteen minutes in the pool. Most good gyms will offer you an induction course. Discuss with the supervisor what you want to get out of going, and together work out some realistic targets. You can always increase your commitment when you feel up to it.

Also, don't rush your sessions. Where before – if you belonged to a gym at all – you were probably racing through your programme because you had someone to go home to, now you've got time on your hands. So, enjoy it. Have a cup of coffee or a glass of fruit juice afterwards. Get chatting to people. Make it an occasion.

But if a gym isn't your bag, why not find out about dance classes, or consider going walking: if you join the Ramblers Association, for example, you'll never be stuck for something to do at weekends, or for someone to talk to.

You may decide on new projects that will improve your mind. Plenty of people decide to do an Open University degree. Again, beware of taking on too much too soon.

Evening classes are usually a good bet and because of the Internet, it's never been easier to find out what's on offer wherever you live. Public libraries are a good source of information too.

Book Groups have become very trendy and they are a perfect diversion for someone who loves reading and would like to meet others with a similar fondness for books. Your nearest bookshop may well have a notice board advertising local book groups, as well as details of book signings and Question and Answer sessions with writers.

Basically, you should aim to enjoy the extra time you've got to yourself. You probably won't be on your own for ever, so make this a productive period in your life for exploring your own interests and ambitions.

There are lots more ideas about filling your single life in Chapter Seventeen.

New You

There's hardly anyone – male or female – who doesn't get into a bit of a rut when they're in a relationship. So when you emerge from a broken romance, this is a very good time to discover a 'new you'.

Most individuals lose weight when they're unhappy – so that takes care of the weight question for many people. But some sort of make-over usually helps you feel much better about yourself. A new hairstyle – whether you're male or female – can take years off you. And shopping for new clothes can do the same.

This needn't be a huge expense. Nowadays, it's chic to get bargains in charity shops. Also, there are discount outlet stores all over the country where you can always get genuine bargains – if you're prepared to give it time to sort through a lot of dross in order to find the finery that will show off the new you.

Christmas

The first Christmas after a relationship ends is usually very miserable. And if you break up shortly before Christmas, it's bound to be very difficult for you. Some individuals love to return to their parents and have a traditional Yuletide and allow themselves to be spoiled. Others can't stand it.

Many people who have ended a relationship have children to consider. For some, Christmas is one of the days when the kids are going to be with their other parent, which is very difficult.

My advice is to indulge yourself as selfishly as possible during this first, difficult Christmas. So far as you are able, do what *you* want to do, and ignore pressures from other people where it's feasible to do so.

Lots of hurt and miserable individuals find it easier to go and help others rather than to try to celebrate when it feels all wrong. If you're in a job where you can elect to work on Christmas Day – you might find that this is your best option. If you're a nurse, for example, or you work in a hotel, your colleagues will be delighted with you if you volunteer to do the Christmas Day shift!

But if you work in an office and it's closed for the holiday, you might consider working for a charity. I know of two divorcees who couldn't face Christmas the first year they were on their own and they signed up to work for the homeless charity, Crisis. They told me that, for the first time in ages, they believed they'd experienced the true spirit of Christmas. They felt useful, wanted and busy and had such a wonderful time that they worked for Crisis again for several more years afterwards – even though they had both found new partners in the meantime.

But opting to do this kind of thing takes some planning, so don't leave it to the last minute, or the chances are that you won't be needed.

Alternatively, there's no actual law that states that you must acknowledge Christmas and its festivities at all. If you hate the idea of going to friends or family, and don't want to celebrate at all, then don't. I know a guy whose girlfriend dumped him in December. He spent Christmas Day re-decorating his flat. He got quite a buzz from it and felt very much better as a result.

Drinking and Smoking

The day your lover leaves you is not the best time to give up smoking! But in the months that follow, it's important to be aware of the dangers of upping your intake of cigarettes, alcohol or leisure drugs.

Most of these things are addictive and, although you may think they're helping you, they can cause more problems than they solve. Of course, you're likely to take refuge in substances such as alcohol, which blur the edges. Most people do – and I was no different at one time. I know what it is to come home – having done your best to act normally throughout the day even though your heart is breaking – and to have poured a whacking great gin and tonic and drunk it, before you've even taken off your coat!

But this is crazy behaviour. Especially when you pour another. If you're getting to the stage where you 'need' a drink to calm you or to cheer you up – you will spend too much time drinking alone, or making false friends in pubs. Furthermore, alcohol will weaken your resolve to do healthy things for yourself and – worst of all – will depress you.

It's a proven fact that the first couple of units of alcohol serve to take away one's inhibitions and to elevate one's mood, but that successive units act as a depressant. A long evening's drinking will not leave you feeling better about yourself or your situation – it might well leave you suicidal.

Too much smoking (of tobacco) may not alter your mood much, but it's also a crazy habit to indulge. It clogs up your lungs, makes you less energetic, much less inclined to go to the gym or to a dance class – and very much less likely to eat or drink healthy foods.

Let's face it, cigarettes go best with loads of coffee, alcohol and comforting foods. They don't mix well with orange juice, mineral water, fruit teas, salads, grilled fish and so on.

I'm not preaching at you – as I say, I've been there. But I am telling you unequivocally that what you're doing is not beneficial. Be aware that *needing* to smoke or drink is not a happy state of affairs.

You might also consider just what your behaviour with alcohol and tobacco is signalling to other people. I have had clients in my consulting room – men and women – who absolutely reek of booze and/or tobacco. And I mean that the smell coming off them is so strong I find it offensive.

Now, I'm someone with quite a strong stomach. I also have a lot of knowledge and understanding of what makes distressed people behave as they do – and I have a lot of sympathy too. But other individuals may well be less tolerant and will interpret your signals as a profound lack of care and respect for yourself – and they will find these signals *very* unattractive.

OK, right now you may not care much what happens to you, or what other people think, but please try to accept that there will come a day when you *will*. And then you may well regret the bad habits you've got yourself into – because they may not only damage your health, but also prevent people who are mentally and physically healthy from wanting to know you.

Sex

Frankly, and you may not want to hear this, the safest, most reliable form of sex while you're still raw and heartbroken is masturbation. You can take your time. You can love your own body in exactly the way it likes, and you can welcome anyone you desire into your fantasies!

I know that plenty of people feel that the best thing to do when you lose a sexual partner is to hop on to the next one that comes along! But anyone can get laid. Being on your own for a bit – nurturing yourself, and working through your pain – is the better, if tougher, option.

Men, in particular, tend to be like victims of a shipwreck. They're all at sea without their woman, and can think of nothing except casting around for the next bit of available driftwood.

This rarely results in a meaningful relationship – although sometimes they marry the 'driftwood' before they realise that they would have done better to wait.

I can think of a guy who was shaken to the core by his wife's desertion and who, in his grief, comforted himself with a distant cousin. Sadly, it was obvious to everyone that they didn't get on, and that he was pandering to her every demand – and there were plenty of those – just because he needed to fill the gap his wife had left.

To his friends' dismay, he got engaged to this woman and planned to marry her, with indecent haste. And when his brother boldly suggested that the new partner was not ideal, he answered: 'I know – but I can't face living alone!'

It's hardly surprising that this relationship failed before the strains of Mendelssohn's *Wedding March* had died away!

Then there were the two sets of married doctors in rival practices. Geoff, from one practice, ran away with Barbara from the other one. Unfortunately, their respective spouses decided to find consolation in each other's company – and they got married as soon as the two divorces came through.

Once they'd got over their hurt, they realised that they had nothing in common – apart from the fact that they were both doctors and that their ex-partners, Geoff and Barbara, had fallen in love.

Moreover, the children of this rather odd form of mixed doubles were very disturbed by these shenanigans, and two of the kids ended up in therapy. Indeed, there was much heartache all round.

You can't really believe that professional people, who understand how the mind and body work, can be so stupid – but unintelligent and ill-educated people do not have the monopoly of strange behaviour after relationships break up!

Then there's the situation where a rejected person opts for a spot of hanky-panky with an old friend. This isn't always disastrous. Sometimes it can feel quite comforting. But, though sex often starts as a no-strings-attached scenario, emotions frequently follow. And you may hurt this old friend – or indeed yourself.

The ultimate in bad behaviour is to have sex with a pal's spouse. Unfortunately, when we are hurting, we tend to think that it's OK to do something this reprehensible. We argue that 'someone did it to us', or that 'I deserve a bit of comfort.'

These are not sufficiently good reasons – and you will probably hate yourself after the act. Furthermore, you will almost certainly lose far more than your frustration. You could easily lose a lifelong friend.

Of course, you may elect to have sex with someone you don't know at all. Plenty of grief-stricken people go clubbing or pull some stranger at a party. And I would be lying if I said that such encounters are always disastrous – because of course they're not. But they can be.

Melanie told me how she picked up a guy in a bar. They had a few drinks and she invited him back to her place. 'This was a slightly risky thing to do, I know,' she said. 'But I was lonely.'

Predictably, while they were making love, she started thinking about her husband who had left her, and she began to cry – and the next thing she knew was that she was hitting the man she'd brought home and screaming at him to get out of her house. She just felt overwhelmed with anger at her husband – and also at the guy, because he *wasn't* her husband.

As it turned out, this bloke was a perfect gentleman. He tried to console her – and then he left, and no harm was done. But things could have turned very ugly, and Melanie realised it – albeit late in the day.

Most of us are really not ready for sex – let alone relationships – during the first few months of heartbreak. It's tough being without a partner, but if you surround yourself with friends, pursue some interesting activities, and nurture and indulge yourself, then the day will come when you'll be ready for a new relationship – for all the right reasons, and not because you simply cannot bear to be alone.

Finally, never, ever be tempted to allow your ex into your bed. Your recovery will greatly suffer if you do. You might feel better – temporarily – but afterwards you'll probably feel used, ashamed, sad, lonelier than ever, and utterly discarded. So, beware of this unwise possibility if, for example, you go back to your old flat to pick up your books and CDs.

Anthony had taken the break-up from Susie very hard indeed. They had been together for four years and he had assumed that – in time – they would marry and have children. But, out of the blue, Susie announced that she had got restless, and she asked Anthony to leave the flat they'd shared.

Six miserable weeks later, Anthony heard from Susie for the first time: she rang to suggest that he came round and cleared out the remains of his stuff. When he arrived, Susie was very welcoming. She opened a bottle of wine while he gathered all his things together. Then, she kissed him. One thing led to another – and they ended up in bed, having very good sex. Anthony was overjoyed. But afterwards, Susie said that nothing had changed – and she still needed time and space to herself.

As he left her flat – having gone through a barrage of emotions – Anthony seriously contemplated throwing himself into the river. By opening himself up to her and by holding her again in his arms, he realised that any progress he had made in the past few weeks had been completely erased – and that he now had to start again.

Another common scenario occurs when you share children. David had walked out on his ten-year-old marriage to be with his secretary. His wife, Claire, had been devastated. But she had gone along with what he had wanted and had tried to be pleasant to him when he returned to pick up the children every Saturday and Sunday.

After a couple of months apart, he brought back the children as usual. Then he suggested coming in to put them to bed. Claire got the feeling that he was missing family life, and part of her thought that by having him back in the house, he might realise what a terrible mistake he'd made in leaving.

So, she helped him put the kids to bed and then she offered him a beer. One beer became several. David seemed concerned for her and put his arm around her and asked if she was coping. She began to cry and the next thing she knew was that he was kissing her and leading her into their old bedroom.

She was thrilled to be in her lover's arms again and made no protest when David initiated sex. Afterwards, he dressed quickly and said: 'This should never have happened.' He sounded cross – as if it was her fault. And then he left her for his new love.

That night she felt worse than she had at any time since learning he'd fallen for someone else. Having sex opened up all her raw emotions, and left her feeling more sad and lonely than ever.

But don't any ex-partners ever realise they've made a mistake, you might ask, and decide they have very genuine reasons for trying to rekindle the relationship? Well, yes they do. But if someone wants to return to the home the two of you once shared and to reignite the relationship, then he or she must 'earn' the right to come back – slowly. There must be much discussion, apology, and an attempt on both sides to understand what happened. Then some gentle courting can begin. This is not the same thing at all as having opportunistic sex – and having no intention of regularising the relationship again.

So, *never have sex with your ex.* Save yourself for someone who will put you on a pedestal and be totally faithful to you, and will make you his or her top priority. You deserve nothing less.

Part Two

Getting Over It

11

What You *Don't* Miss

As we begin Part Two of this book, I'd like you to double-check that Part One is working for you:

- Have you got over your shock?
- Are you taking care of your physical wellbeing?
- Are you letting other people care for you?
- Are you in touch with your own goodness?
- Have you assessed where the responsibility lies for the end of the relationship?
- Have you stopped seeing your ex – as far as is humanly possible?
- If you're a parent, are you coping with what your children need to know – and have you got some sort of mediation set up with your former partner?
- Are you actively pursuing new interests, avoiding sex with unsuitable people, very definitely *not* having sex with your ex, and getting yourself in shape, both physically and mentally?

If you can say 'yes' to the vast majority of these questions, then give yourself a pat on the back. However, if you're saying 'no' to more than three of them, I suggest you reread the first part of the book before continuing.

OK, now we're going to get this process of recovery underway by assessing what it is about your partner that you *don't* miss. This is a very good exercise for anyone emerging from a relationship.

If you were the partner who ended it, this assessment can be of great help – especially in those wee small lonely hours when you wonder if your old relationship would be better than none. And if you were the rejected one, it can help you too – because it will start you thinking hard about what the relationship really had in it for *you*.

When we've been dumped, we tend to view our ex-lover through rose-tinted specs. This doesn't help us get over it.

In Chapter Six, I encouraged you to examine the quality of your relationship in comparison with what I regard to be a good and compatible romantic partnership. And I hope that, by now, you have a pretty realistic view of your life together.

But in this chapter, we're going to take things a stage further. I'm going to ask you to get really personal about your ex, and to identify all the things about him or her that you disliked.

To do this, I want you to compile a list of all the things about your ex that you *do not miss*. You can start it right now, if you like, while you are reading this chapter.

And just in case you're still stuck with the notion that he or she was perfect, or 'the love of your life', take a deep breath and allow yourself to remember it as it *really* was.

On close examination, most heartbroken individuals will accept that there *were* things about their ex that they didn't like at all. These characteristics might not have been so awful that they made the relationship completely untenable, but even so, they were probably pretty annoying.

For instance, many women dislike how their mates surf through the television channels instead of looking up what's on in the TV Guide. Lots of men hate being dragged around women's clothes shops and being asked: 'Do I look fat in this?' Many women dislike their men's passion for sport. And virtually all females hate the way men leave the lavatory seat up!

Irritations like these are not very likely to have been the root cause of your break up – but if they strike a chord with you, they should go on your list when you start it.

Now think a little deeper. Perhaps your ex was:

- grumpy;
- unpredictable;
- forever putting you down;
- dreadfully untidy;
- keen to try and change you;
- terrified of commitment;
- horrid to your friends and/or family;
- resentful if you had to work late;
- mean;
- huffy if sex wasn't always on the menu;
- nasty about your cooking;
- fond of telling the same, old, terrible jokes at parties.

Do some of these strike home? Put on your list any that are true. Once you've got started, you'll think of plenty more.

You might remember Anna whom I wrote about in Chapter Two. She was the one who finally ended a marriage in which she had to do everything, and which had been very hard work for years. Here's her list:

Anna's 'What I Don't Miss' List

1 His laziness.
2 His lack of direction in life.
3 His moodiness.
4 His lack of sex drive in recent months.

5 The way he was prone to get drunk – and angry – if we ever had dinner with any of my friends.

6 The fact that he rarely left the house – so I never got any time or space there on my own.

7 The fact that he always assumed that I would pay the household bills.

8 His refusal to even try to get on with my family.

9 The way he always assumed that I would be the first to make up any quarrel.

10 His nastiness to me when I finally broke up with him.

That was quite a list – and I know that Anna added to it when new things occurred to her over a period of about six months. But, as we know, it was Anna who ended the marriage. And you may therefore not be too surprised by her catalogue of woes.

But what sort of list can you make if you worshipped the ground your lover walked on – and he or she rejected *you*?

Well, it's true that in those circumstances your ex-partner's faults may not seem so horrendous.

Gary was someone else I wrote about in Chapter Two. He was the one who was utterly devastated, and in a terrible mental and physical state when his girlfriend finished with him. We'll look at his list next. It took longer to compile than Anna's, because initially he swore that his ex was so wonderful he would miss *everything* about her.

However, gradually he realised that this wasn't true at all. There had been quite a lot of problems in the relationship and, bit by bit, he started to face up to all the things that had disappointed him.

Gary's 'What I Don't Miss' List

1 She didn't like me to be affectionate to her in company.

2 She used to put her friends before me.

3 I felt she used to just squeeze me into her crowded schedule.
4 She was always cutting our dates short by saying she had to get an early night before work.
5 She would very rarely come to my house – I always had to go to hers.
6 She expected me to like her sort of music, but made no effort to listen to the sort I like.
7 I felt her job came before me.
8 She used to ridicule me.
9 I don't think she respected me.
10 She seemed to delight in disagreeing with me.
11 She made very little effort to get on with my circle of friends.
12 She had a much lower sex drive than me.
13 When she was ill, I took time off work and looked after her – but she never looked after me.
14 She thought the sort of holidays that I enjoy are boring.

This list took Gary about a week to write. But afterwards, he pinned it up on his kitchen noticeboard and added to it from time to time. He was amazed at how much he had actually disliked about his girlfriend and about his relationship.

In fact, as a result, he could see that although he had adored and idolised his ex, the relationship had never been sound.

And this leads us to a very important point in the recovery process. As I said in Chapter Six, sometimes we have to admit that it's not so much that the relationship has gone *wrong*, but rather that there was never anything very *right* about it.

Of course, when we're locked into the fond idea that we've just lost the love of our life, it's hard to face up to the realisation that the relationship had little going for it. But when we *can* face that, we begin to recover.

Kate, whom we last met in Chapter Nine, was forced to admit that her long affair with her college lecturer lover had been a mistake when her lover finally left his wife – not for her, but for someone new. She was distraught and angry by his betrayal, but writing her list was still difficult because, in order to do it, she had to face up to the fact that she had kept herself in a relationship that demeaned her. Here's her list:

Kate's 'What I Don't Miss' List

1 Being taken up and put down to fit in with his schedule – not mine.
2 The way he used to get depressed – and withdraw from me.
3 Never celebrating Christmas, New Year or his birthday together.
4 Not being able to depend on him to see me on *my* birthday.
5 His insistence that I keep our affair secret from my family and friends.
6 His meanness – in the latter years he never took me out, just came to my place for dinner and sex.
7 He could be very sneering about my opinions.
8 He put me down any time he suspected I was thinking of changing jobs or moving away – this was his way of keeping me, I suspect.
9 His refusal to make a regular date with me – again this kept me hanging on and often I would stay in, just in case he got free and was able to pop round.
10 The way he would fondle me intimately without even kissing me when he turned up – it made me feel cheap and as if all he wanted was sex in a hurry.
11 When we *did* go out, his eyes used to swivel around the room looking at other women. He always claimed I imagined this, but I know I didn't.

Kate's list grew and grew in the weeks following the end of the affair. And the more she wrote down, the more depressed she became about herself.

'How could I have put up with all of this for so long?' she asked me.

Well, he was a habit. Perhaps in the early days he was a good habit – although that's questionable – but in the latter years, the habit was definitely a bad one.

Writing down what you don't miss is a very good exercise that will help you see your ex-lover for what he or she really was. But it can make you feel much worse – before you feel better – because it does raise the issue of what on earth you were *doing* with this person.

Try to accept that you can't change the past, but that you can change how you *think* about it. When you've done that, you can help yourself to think differently from now on. You can also vow not to repeat the mistakes of your last relationship, when you get into a new one. And this is a crucial point: how many people do you know who always seem to go for the same type of partner, and who seem to endlessly repeat the same mistakes in relationships every time? I know a lot – and perhaps you do too.

Facing up to your ex's bad points – and to what you put up with for far too long – is a positive step towards becoming an adult who learns from a bad relationship and is therefore in a good position to form a healthier one *next* time.

So, now that you've read Anna's and Gary's and Kate's lists, draw up your own.

Don't worry if it takes you a while. You can put down a few things today and gradually add to it over the next few weeks.

As I said earlier, start with trivial things and the more serious ones will gradually bubble up into your mind.

You may well feel uncomfortable as it takes shape. Like Kate, you may begin to despair. Seeing what was wrong with the relationship in black and white can prove very depressing reading.

But do remember that while you were in the relationship, you were thinking differently from how you are starting to think now. You can't rewrite what happened at that time, or how you thought then. All you can do is to start being different from now on.

So don't blame yourself. That was then. This is now.

12

What You *Do* Miss

In Chapter Eleven, I encouraged you to compile a list of everything you don't miss about your ex-partner. No matter how long that list becomes, there may be times when you will miss your ex so desperately that you will almost certainly find yourself in real physical pain. This pain is often in the chest, near the heart, and I suppose that is why we refer to ourselves as having 'heartache' or as being 'heartbroken'.

I can certainly remember the first time I got this pain. I felt as though my whole torso were being crushed by a giant clamp or vice and I could hardly breathe. I was only seventeen at the time, and I had nothing to compare it with. For days I thought I must be physically ill. And all because I had convinced myself that I was passionately in love with someone who hardly knew I was alive!

Well, I can smile at my seventeen-year-old self now. But, from a much older vantage point – and a very much happier one – I can see that everything I went through in my younger years contributed to my finding the peace and contentment I have today.

However, I know that the pain I had was real, even though

it started in my mind and was not a symptom of a physical illness. And I have never, ever forgotten it.

You may well be experiencing pain that is just as excruciating now. And when you get it, you're bound to say: 'I really, really miss him' or: 'I need her so much, I'll never get over losing her.'

So, in this chapter, we're going to look at exactly *what* you miss. Before you quickly and indignantly turn over the page – because, of course, you know exactly what you miss and why – please give me time to explain.

When we end a relationship, we do, as you have read in Chapter One, make things worse by confusing the loss we feel now with an erroneous belief that things will never get better in the future. That confusion adds to our pain. If you don't remember that bit, have a look back at the beginning of the book and reread it.

Well, just as we make things worse by confusing our current loss with predicted endless loss in the future, we are often very confused about how or why we miss someone. Or, to put it another way, by what we *really* miss about them.

You see, the truth is that what we're missing is often not so much that person who was in our life, but the experience of being in a relationship.

We miss:

- being loved;
- having someone to love;
- being part of a couple;
- the memory of good days rather than a realistic recall of the whole thing;
- having someone to come home to;
- having someone to go to parties with;
- being settled.

To explain this further, let's take a look at what Anna and Gary and Kate missed about their relationships when I asked them to write me a list.

Anna's 'What I Do Miss' List

1 Being in a relationship.
2 Having someone to cuddle up to on cold evenings.
3 Knowing what I'm going to be doing at Christmas.
4 Believing that my relationship would go on.
5 The possibility of having children with him.
6 Being wanted.
7 Being depended upon.
8 The sex – he *was* good at that even though we didn't do it very often.
9 Having someone to spend Sundays with.
10 Having someone to discuss the day with – although in recent years, he wasn't very interested in what I did.
11 Laughing together – in the early days, we found the same things very funny.
12 Feeling that I was in love – although I haven't felt that for a long time.
13 The familiarity of living with someone you've known for a long time.
14 Having someone to believe in – because I did believe he was a talented person, and that I could help him to make something of himself.

Does anything strike you about Anna's list? Can you see that what she was missing didn't have much to do with the man she'd left, but rather more to do with being without a loving relationship? Of course, Anna had chosen to end the relationship, and by the time someone does that, they're often very fed up indeed with their partner.

Neither Gary nor Kate chose to end their relationships. They were dumped. So let's take a look at what they said they missed:

Gary's 'What I Do Miss' List

1 Her smile.
2 Her body.
3 The lovely smell of her.
4 The feel of her arms around me.
5 Having sex – even though it happened rarely and I was never sure she enjoyed it.
6 Being part of a couple, as it gave me confidence.
7 Planning what to do at bank holidays, and Christmas, knowing that it would involve her.
8 Pottering around markets on Sundays.
9 Having someone special in my life.
10 Knowing who I would take to any party that came up.
11 How we used to talk for hours together – in the early days.
12 Feeling more of a success as a person when I was in a relationship.

Kate's 'What I Do Miss' List

1 Having someone special.
2 Being loved and adored – which I certainly was by him in the early days.
3 Being listened to – again, this didn't happen much in recent years, but when I was his student, he used to make me feel bright and clever and capable, and that made me feel important.
4 Sex – it became a bit routine in the latter years but we did have very good chemistry and he knew how to make me orgasm.
5 The excitement: affairs are secret and that has its drawbacks, but they have a sort of 'danger', which is exciting.
6 Feeling that I had someone special of my own – even though, of course, he was never really mine and I shared him with his wife, and maybe others.

7 Looking after him: he often seemed like a little boy and I used to love taking care of him and giving him lemon and honey, for example, if he had a bad cold.

8 Having someone to focus on – whatever I did, I always had him in the back of my mind.

9 Romantic weekends away – admittedly these only happened five times in seventeen years, but in the early days, when he used to go off to Summer Schools, he took me with him.

10 He used to recommend books I might like to read.

Well, what do you make of that? And how similar are these lists to one that you might write?

Before you write yours, can I suggest you look again at Anna's and Gary's and Kate's lists. I think it would be useful if you added up how many of the points in each case were specifically about the missed *person* – and how many of the points were about missing having *someone*, or simply missing being in a relationship.

Anna wrote down fourteen things about her ex-husband that she missed. Frankly, I think all fourteen could be about the experience of having *someone* rather than about the *man* she was married to.

But, at a pinch, you could say that Numbers 4, 8, 10, 11, 12 and 14 were connected with her husband as opposed to any old bloke. Though I'm sure you'd agree that most of the things she misses about him she also admits are things that haven't happened for a while.

How many of the things which Gary misses are specifically to do with his previous girlfriend? Well, I make it five out of his twelve. And I think I'm being generous! In my view, the points that are about *her* as opposed to any woman he might have a relationship with are Numbers: 1, 2, 3, 4, 8 and 11.

And finally, let's look at what Kate misses. She wrote down ten points and I think that most of them could apply to any decent bloke that she might have been involved with, rather than being specifically about her long-term lecturer lover.

But I am prepared to agree that Numbers 3, 4, 5, 7, 9 and 10 could all have *something* to do with the man himself rather than simply the experience of being in a loving relationship. However, I'm sure you can see that some of the things she misses are to do with the relationship as it was in the early days – and not recently.

Now we come to you. I'd like you to make your own list of what you miss.

Of course, I've alerted you to the fact that people usually write down a load of stuff about relationships in general as opposed to specifics about their lost love – and you may therefore strive to make yours very personal. But take your time and, as you write, ask yourself whether what you're writing applies strictly to the person you have lost, or whether it could just as easily apply to anyone you might have a relationship with.

I don't think you'll be able to complete this task now, or even today. It could take weeks. But don't give up on it. Quite apart from anything else, it will help you to see more clearly what you most value in a relationship.

When you have a list which seems complete, it might be interesting for you to compare it with Anna's and Gary's and Kate's lists.

It will also help you to compare it with the final list in this chapter, which was compiled by a fifty-year-old woman called Cassie.

She and her husband have a very happy and compatible relationship which has lasted almost twenty years. I asked her to write down for me exactly what she would miss *if* her relationship, through some tragedy, ended today.

Here's what she put:

Cassie's 'What I Would Miss' List

1 Waking up every morning and immediately feeling loved and affirmed.
2 The feel of his body as he curls round my bottom when we go to sleep.
3 The way he tells me he loves me about fifty times a day.
4 His loving phone calls several times a day.
5 His laugh.
6 His body.
7 His smile.
8 The way he talks about me on the phone to his family and friends – proudly and lovingly.
9 The way he looks after me.
10 Great sex.
11 Watching rugby with him.
12 Eating out – we seem to have so much to talk about even after being together for twenty years.
13 Going to the opera together – because he loves it and knows so much about it.
14 Going to the theatre together – he really throws himself into it, and I like the fact that he is very appreciative of the effort made by the actors.
15 Playing tennis together.
16 Going to France together – he speaks really good French, which I always find impressive!
17 The way he agrees with my political views and listens to them.
18 The way he appreciates my mind.
19 The fact that he still finds me sexy after all this time.
20 His intelligence.
21 The way he loves to watch murder-mysteries on the television with me – and really gets into them.
22 His love of romantic comedies.
23 The way we just enjoy the companionship of being together.

If you look closely at what Cassie would miss, you'll see that virtually all her points are about her husband – and not about some vague experience of any relationship.

This contrasts very clearly with Anna's and Gary's and Kate's lists, don't you agree? And I think it will be rather different from your list too.

This is just a small example of what I have found through the years when trying to help people with their relationships.

When two people are compatible and in love with each other, they are able to value each other for who and what they *really* are – and not for some vague fantasy.

But when people are in the wrong relationship – or in a relationship that is failing – they tend to ignore their partner's faults and to overstate what they are getting from the other person.

I hope you are seeing your past partner – and your past relationship – more clearly and more realistically than you used to.

13

Setting the Record Straight

After the last two chapters, you should be seeing your past relationship rather differently and perhaps more realistically. You may even have come to the conclusion that it was quite bad for you, or that it had become a bad habit. But you will still have days where it will feel like unfinished business.

At this stage, even when people can acknowledge the flaws in their ex and in their former romance, they often have a burning desire to set the record straight.

They say things like:

- It's time to tell her exactly what she's done to me.
- I want to make her realise how much I loved her.
- I'm going to tell him he's treated me like dirt.
- I want him to know that I'll always love him.
- I need him to know how ill he's made me.
- I want him to know that just because he's being financially generous – that *doesn't* make everything OK.
- I want to have my say about the end of the relationship – at

the time, he just told me he was dumping me and then he
left.

So, if you have these sorts of feelings, what should you do
about them? First of all, I have to tell you that in the majority
of cases, your ex *does* know what you want to impart. He *does*
know that you love him more than life itself. She *does* know
that she is your ideal woman and you've never fancied anyone
in the same way. He *does* know – if rather deep down – that
he's been unfair in telling you he was leaving as he roared
away in his car.

As for talking it out, well, when I see couples in trouble, the
man invariably says: 'All we do is drone on about our problems
over and over again.' While the woman usually says: 'We never
talk about this.'

They can't both be right! But they *think* they are, and their
perceptions of what happens behind closed doors often remain
very different. So, is there much point in setting the record
straight? At this stage in your recovery, I think there *is* a case
for writing down everything that happened in the relationship
and during its demise, and then, if you want to, sending it
to your former partner. This can help you from a cathartic
and therapeutic point of view. But don't expect it to evoke a
complete change of heart in your ex – because it won't.

But if you *are* going to set the record straight in this way,
how should you do it? Is a letter better than an email or a
phone call? I think it is. But that is not to say you should
definitely send it. Sometimes, having written down the whole
story as they see it, people feel more able to put it behind them
– and they never send the letter. This is one solution. But if you
can't see the point of doing it *without* sending it, what should
you remember?

The crucial point is that this is a one-off. This is not
reopening dialogue. If your ex chooses to write back, that is
their own business, but you are writing to have your say, once
and for all.

Your letter, then, must differ from any that flew backwards and forwards during the 'accepting it' phase. This should be a well-thought-out document which calmly and assertively puts over your point of view.

Personally, I don't believe you should even begin to construct such a letter until you have been apart for at least three months. And I think you have to be very careful to be sure that your motive in writing is to draw a line under the relationship rather than to persuade your ex to come back to you.

Many individuals write to their ex, believing that, by putting their side of the story, their loved one will realise that ending the relationship has been a massive mistake – and will return.

Be honest with yourself. If you know that you are still hoping that by making contact you might get back together with your ex – then you still haven't really accepted that the relationship is over. Until you do, you shouldn't write the 'set the record straight' letter.

If you go ahead nonetheless – and sadly, plenty of people do – you will only reopen your unhealed wound. And, every day, you're going to be waiting for the postman, holding your breath and looking out for that kind and contrite reply. Don't do this to yourself. You've started to recover. Don't do anything that will cause a relapse.

But, assuming you have accepted the end of the relationship, albeit reluctantly, then it may well help you to write the letter putting your point of view, even though you may eventually decide not to send it.

So what should go into this letter? Well, since it's a one-off, I think that you should put down everything that you want to say. For this reason, regard the writing of the letter as a major undertaking. You should take at least a fortnight over it. It is better written sober – though you'll be a saint if you achieve this! But those bits that are written under the influence of anything other than tea, coffee or soft drinks should be keenly scrutinised before they're allowed to form part of the final text.

Most importantly, if you have children, bear in mind that there's always a chance that they will see this letter. So don't commit anything to paper that would shock or disturb them. For example, Greg was very hostile towards his ex-wife. He felt used. He was broke because of the divorce and he couldn't see how he could survive in his bedsit, let alone get himself together to ever meet anyone else. But his biggest gripe was that he thought his wife had only married him in order to have children – and that the only times in their marriage that she'd shown interest in sex was when she had wanted to conceive.

He felt duped and decided he'd been treated like a baby-making machine, so he put all this down in his letter. The words: 'used me like a f****** sperm bank' featured prominently. He also said that he had been forced into 'making' their two sons, and had not felt ready to be a father.

His wife – probably deliberately – left the letter around, and Greg's ten- and eight-year-old sons found and read it. Greg was already struggling to form a new relationship with the kids, and only got to see them on Sundays and for half of the holidays – occasions that, so far, had seemed difficult and strained.

Having seen his letter to their mother, however, they concluded that he'd never really wanted them – and the relationship between Greg and his sons suffered enormously.

Of course, Greg truly loved his kids and showed them this in masses of ways. But they were very upset to learn about his reluctance to become a dad, and also of the hostile feelings he held for their mother. And this new-found information damaged the father-sons relationship at a time when it was already fragile.

So, yet again, people with broken hearts who have children should put their kids first. It's difficult. It might feel unfair. But the alternative – which is that they learn stuff about you and your ex that no child should be asked to cope with – is infinitely worse. To return to *your* letter – what do you want to put in it?

Obviously you are feeling hurt, sad – and maybe ignored. These are good things to explain. You might have some issues about promises that were blithely made, but never honoured. You may feel that you were 'put down' in the relationship. You may want your ex to know that sex was never great. You may feel strongly that this person never tried to understand your ambition, or your family ties, or even how much effort you put into sustaining the relationship. This can go into the letter.

But, do remember that too much hostility or hysteria will probably result in your missive being binned before your ex gets to some of the important points. And if you want this communication to be seriously considered, it will help if you write down some of the things that *you* might have handled better, rather than focusing exclusively on everything that your ex did wrong.

When you have finished, my advice is to keep your letter for another couple of weeks, and then to look at it again. At that stage, you may decide to add more to it, or to erase some of the paragraphs.

And then what? Actually, as I said earlier, many individuals surprise themselves at this point by deciding that they don't need to send the letter. They may put it away among their souvenirs of the relationship, or they may destroy it in some sort of 'last ceremony' – some people bury their letter and others set fire to them in the garden.

One woman I know came to the conclusion – having written her letter – that the relationship had been so damaging to her, she wanted to discard it somewhere really horrible. As it happens, her town had recently been flooded and there were rubbish skips all over the place, filled with smelly, damp and rotting carpets and furniture that the flood victims had been forced to dump. She found the one that looked and smelt worst and pushed her letter into it.

Another woman went walking on the Sussex Downs on a very windy day and she tore her letter into tiny fragments and scattered them in the breeze. They were swept away by gusts of up to seventy miles an hour and she claimed to feel quite liberated in that moment – as if her old life were being blown away, leaving her ready for a new one.

There is no right or wrong way of dealing with your letter. All I would advise is that you take your time and make sure you're doing what you really want to do.

Finally, it may occur to you that you'd like to 'set the record straight' with other people connected with your ex – such as his or her parents, other family members or long-term friends. Perhaps you and his mum got on fantastically well. Maybe you used to go to the football with her brother. Perhaps his oldest pal spent all your marriage telling you that you were 'too good for the old bastard'. Or maybe your ex's closest friend used to take your side in arguments.

All these sorts of situations can lead you to suppose that your ex's nearest and dearest will not only be horrified that you have split up, but will also be on 'your side'.

Don't make this mistake! It will only lead to disappointment. When the end comes, usually no one from 'the other side' is interested in hearing a laundry list of faults of one of their own. And the chances are that even though you thought you were all great mates, no one will want to know you after the break-up.

There are exceptions to this stance of course – especially if your ex was actually physically violent to you, or was convicted of some awful crime like rape or murder. But, apart from that, you'll find that his or her side will close ranks – just as your side is probably doing the same for you.

If you have children, it is likely that your in-laws will want to maintain contact with them – and in most cases it is absolutely right that they should. After all, grandparents shouldn't be divorced along with a partner, and kids should not suddenly be deprived of grandparents. But even so, you'll find that your ex's parents' attitudes to *you* will probably change, even if they're anxious to keep a good relationship going with your children.

Philippa had always got on fantastically well with her mother-in-law but when her husband had an affair – an affair that finally ended the marriage – Philippa found that the friendship with his mother didn't survive.

This caused pain to both women, but as the mother-in-law said: 'He's my son. I don't want any rift with him, so I have to accept his new partner. And I can't really do that and still go out for a drink or to the theatre with you.'

I know this doesn't sound or feel very fair, but I can assure you that it is what happens most of the time. So it is pointless pouring your heart out to someone close to your ex. They will almost certainly be embarrassed about it. They may even refuse to listen, or to read anything you write about the relationship – which might leave you feeling even more rejected than you do already.

Occasionally, one of your ex's friends may seem to be on your side, but that usually only happens when they fancy you.

Basically, in the face of a relationship break-up, the blood tie is enormously strong. As for friends, well, nowadays you have to regard anyone's network of friends as being as strong a support as his or her family – often more so. Relationships come and go but your real friends stay with you through life.

Therefore you should not expect one of his or her network to be on your side. They may privately feel you've been let down or betrayed or ill-used, but that probably won't break up the friendship they've had for years with your ex.

So, if you want to tell someone – other than your partner – all about the flaws in the relationship and the unjust treatment you received, save it for your *own* family and friends, who will support you and probably lap up every detail. That's what they're for!

14

How Unhealthy Thinking Maintains Your Misery

This is a rather different chapter. But, in some ways, it's the most important one in the book.

By this stage in your recovery, you probably feel you have tried – or are trying – to do all the right things:

- you've nurtured yourself;
- you've talked endlessly about the break-up with friends;
- you've done your best to sever all contact with your ex;
- if you're a parent, you've sorted out who has the children and how much access each parent is to have;
- you've tried to focus on what you *don't* miss in your former partner;
- you've tried to work out what you actually miss about your partner, as opposed to what you miss about being in *any* loving relationship;
- you've written the 'set the record straight' letter.

So, how do you feel? Hopefully, you feel considerably better than you did, and you're well on your way to putting your heartbreak behind you. But what if you're *not*? What if – despite all your best endeavours – you still feel lousy? What if – although your brain has accepted it's time to move on – you still feel that your normal, happy life has ground to a halt and is definitely not picking up?

I must warn you that if this is happening to you, you're going through a dangerous time – because the feelings you have may encourage you to go back on various good intentions.

If, for example, you've chosen to give up a long–term, clandestine affair which was going nowhere, you might well decide that being a part-time lover was actually better than the isolation you're now experiencing. This thought might then lead you to think that you might as well meet up for a drink and a bit of sex. It might cheer you up, you'll decide, and surely it wouldn't hurt . . .

But it *will* hurt. And it could well put back your recovery by months. Initially, of course, your lover may accept you back joyously and will probably be very attentive and grateful; in fact, there'll be a sort of honeymoon period. But it won't last. Gradually you will begin to sense, yet again, how hopeless it is to be in an affair – and how demeaning it is for you. And then you'll have to make the break all over again.

But what if you were the one who was dumped from a relationship? During this uneasy time you might decide that you'll take up your ex's offer of friendship. So perhaps you'll go out for an evening together. But, as the evening progresses, you'll realise that nothing's changed. This person you've loved so much is certainly *not* asking you to take them back and has very definitely moved on. All that's being offered to you is occasional friendship – but you still want more. And you'll feel the hurt of this rejection all over again. You'll probably also decide that you're truly pathetic and that no one else will ever want you and that he or she was the great love of your life . . . And all those irrational and painful thoughts will resurface and you'll feel worse than you have for months.

So, how should you deal with the fact that you still regret the end of the relationship, you still feel miserable, and you don't feel ready to embrace a new life? The truth is that if you are doing all the right things and you still don't feel better, then it's not so much your situation that is holding you back, it's what you're *thinking*.

Let me explain. Way back in the first century AD, a man called Epictetus (one of the Stoic philosophers) identified a very important idea in mental-health terms. He worked out that:

It's our specific VIEW of a situation that may upset us: it's not the situation itself. In other words, it's our own individual response to events that determines how we handle the events – and how we get over them.

To illustrate this point, let's take one particular circumstance and see how different people view it. We'll look at four friends: they're all female, all of similar intelligence, all studying psychology, all in their final year, and all at the same university.

One day, they learn that their lecturer has had a heart attack and won't be able to teach them for the rest of the academic year. Various other lecturers – none of whom is as senior as their usual one – will cover their classes for a few weeks while the university tries to appoint a locum lecturer with suitable qualifications and experience. But it doesn't seem likely that the administration will be able to get anyone for at least a couple of months.

So how do these four friends respond to this situation?

Emily thinks: 'God! Why do these things keep happening to *me*? Life's always a bloody struggle, and I'm not finding this course at all easy. I'm bound to fail now.'

Vicki thinks: 'What a terrible thing to happen to that poor man. He's only forty-two. I hope he makes a good recovery. We must work hard and get good results as a tribute to him. Thankfully, I'm doing really well with my studies this year, and I'll just have to make sure I continue to do so – even though this is going to cause quite a lot of disruption.'

Jo thinks: 'This is typical of this awful university. They've made so many financial and personnel cutbacks that when something unpredictable happens, they've got no one spare on the staff to help out. Bloody hell! I'm working myself into the ground doing a part-time job to pay my way through the course, and now I'm not going to get value for that money. It's really annoying. They shouldn't be allowed to get away with it.'

Jatinder thinks: 'I suppose I should care, but I never liked that man. I don't wish him dead . . . exactly. But things have got to get better. He never liked me. He made me feel stupid. Whoever we get will be an improvement.'

So, although the situation was identical for these four people their responses were all different. But what, you might ask, is this to do with getting over a relationship? Basically, the story of these four young women shows us that Epictetus was right! It is our view of things that upsets us rather than the situation itself. And this is especially true in the fraught and complex issue of heartbreak.

You have brought your own baggage, your own rules for living, and your own deeply held beliefs to every relationship. And your personal baggage, rules and beliefs have affected the running of your relationship – and now that it is over, these things are determining how you get over your broken heart, as opposed to how other individuals might get over theirs.

Your view of what has happened to you is the crucial factor in your recovery. And the purpose of this chapter is to help you sort out *how* you view your situation so that you can then rethink that view, if necessary, and get on with recovering from your misery.

Put more simply, we need to find out what it is in your *thinking* that is stopping you from getting over the end of your relationship.

To do this, we have to sort out what some of your beliefs about yourself are. What you think about yourself. And what sorts of rules you've made through the years in response to the way your life's gone.

Doing this will impact not only on your current sadness, but it will help you in the future – because if you can learn to think in a more rational and mentally healthy way, this will benefit everything that you do in life.

Let's look at some examples of the way we think which can impede us when we're struggling to get over our heartbreak:

Thinking That Other People MAKE Us Feel Things

We use the term 'made me feel' all the time. We say: 'I missed the train, which made me feel miserable all day.' But in fact, we have a choice about whether – when we miss the train – we're miserable all day or not. Of course it's annoying. But we don't *have* to be miserable. We can *choose* not to be.

You may have noticed that one of the four students I used as an example of how people have differing views in identical situations said: 'He made me feel stupid.' That's a very common expression.

Someone with better self-esteem would say: 'He didn't rate me very much' rather than 'He made me feel stupid.' This is because people with good self-esteem don't allow others to downgrade them in that way.

During relationships, we tend to use the 'make me feel' construction a lot of the time: 'He makes me happy', 'She makes me feel unconfident', 'He makes me feel inferior', 'She makes me feel special' . . . This kind of thinking doesn't do us any favours.

It is my belief that nowadays we should all learn to be as self-reliant as possible. We live in a very flexible, fluid society in which life is increasingly uncertain. We move around the country, move abroad, change careers several times in a lifetime – and often change relationships too. For all these reasons, I think it is better to regard ourselves as an independent person at all times – even during a relationship – so that we always feel responsible for our own life, our own thoughts, feelings and so on.

You might find it rather difficult to see things in this way, but I encourage you to try. I'm not saying, by the way, that you won't feel happier when you're in a lovely relationship than you do now. It's highly probable that you will. But you should not look to a relationship – any relationship – to *make* you happy. If you *do*, you're almost always going to be disappointed. You see, if you believe that you need any relationship or any person to *make* you happy, you put enormous strain on the whole situation, because you believe that without the relationship and that person you are bound to be *unhappy* and that life will be utterly dreadful.

If you wail 'He made me feel so happy', the chances are that you are also telling yourself that you cannot feel happy again while you remain *without* him. Or perhaps that you cannot feel happy again till you have someone else.

Either way, it's nonsense. Even if your ex was fantastic, do you honestly believe that he or she had such a unique skill to elevate your mood that no one out of the world's six billion population can ever do it again? This is rubbish.

And if you mean that you cannot feel special again till someone else comes along and 'makes' you feel special, you are in effect declaring that you cannot feel happy in yourself when you're with friends, or alone, or when you're achieving something great at work – or even when you see the sun setting over the sea.

In such moments I would hope that you would experience pleasure and choose to be happy. If you don't choose happiness at these times, then you're opting out of having a full life.

And what about the words 'She made me feel special'? The downside of this, of course, is that *without* her, you don't feel special at all. In fact, what you're saying to yourself is that you're not very lovable, or that you don't like or love yourself very much.

The answer to this way of thinking – which is very negative – is not simply to get her back, or to get someone just like her, but to learn to value yourself more. Then, any new and lovely person who comes into your life will *enhance* your good feelings about yourself, but he or she won't *make* you feel special, because you'll feel special already! Do you see?

You may think that it's too difficult to change how you think. Well, it *is* difficult. But it's worth it. You wouldn't be reading this book if your life and your emotions were in great shape, so while they're not, it's really worth working on healthy, rational thinking. This will benefit you for ever.

Bridget had a succession of relationships. In each one, she felt special for a while, but then the man in question started to 'make her unhappy'. And when that happened, she became increasingly miserable and eventually the relationship ended – and usually it was her partner who ended it. This cycle seemed worryingly predictable and as the years went on, she became more and more anxious about being single and alone.

It took her a while to see that she was expecting someone else to wave a magic wand over her life and to make it wonderful. And it took even longer to see that if she was unhappy with someone, she actually had the power to change things.

But, one day, she was going to the cinema with her current man, who was acting rather childishly and seemed to be in a bad mood. He was walking ahead of her, refusing to talk to her, and she was trotting behind him wondering what on earth she had done *this* time – and feeling those familiar feelings of rising panic that the relationship might end and she'd be alone again.

Suddenly, she realised what she was doing to herself. She could see – for the first time – that she tended to assume that she had to go along with whatever her man was *making* her feel. She also realised that she tended to put up with *anything* rather than stand up for herself and risk the chance of the relationship ending.

She stopped. He carried on walking. She waited. He still appeared not to have noticed that she was no longer with him. She found herself smiling – then she turned around and walked back to her house.

'I'm worth more than this,' she told herself. 'I am a nice and decent person. I don't deserve this kind of treatment, and I'm not going to put up with it. I don't want the relationship to end – but it won't be the end of the world if it does. And it would be preferable to be single rather than to spend my life being afraid of his moods and of putting my foot wrong all the time.'

She felt a bit shaky and nervous, but at the same time she also felt quite a glow of achievement that, for the first time in her life, she had stopped acting the part of a doormat and had chosen how to feel, rather than have her feelings imposed upon her.

Her man texted her several times that night, but she ignored all his messages. When they met the next day, she explained calmly and assertively that she was not unsympathetic to his problems, but that she was not prepared to be given the silent treatment for no reason – and that if he was unhappy about something he should say so.

This was a real triumph for her. Previously she would have continued on her path to the cinema. She would have put up with his silence, but she would very definitely not have enjoyed the film and would have told herself that he was 'making' her unhappy.

She chose *not* to be unhappy that night. It was a strange feeling – but a good one.

So, have a think about this. Do you believe that other people have the power to *make* you feel unhappy, sad, miserable, happy, complete and so on?

If you do, this suggests to me that you don't have sufficient self-esteem. You see yourself as someone who has no real say about yourself – because you feel that other people always have very strong powers over you. In other words, you see yourself as some kind of a victim. Are your own thoughts turning you into a victim? Are you giving other people responsibility for your thoughts and feelings? If you are, then you are making your heartbreaking situation worse than it needs to be – and I suggest that you get cracking right away on tackling your lack of self-esteem before you get into another relationship.

There are many ways you can do this: for a start, there are plenty of good self-esteem manuals on the market. Or you might want to consider an assertiveness class, which will help you to begin thinking more responsibly and more positively. You might even go for counselling.

You will find useful details on books and classes in the Help Yourself Directory at the back of this book.

Thinking That *Anything*'s Better Than Being Single

Another indication of poor self-esteem is the belief that many people have – and one that Bridget used to have – that they can't be happy if they are not in a relationship.

Do you believe this? Do you perhaps believe that you're a lesser person if you're single? If you do, then getting over heartbreak is going to be extraordinarily difficult.

In other words, it's your own *thinking* about being single, rather than the *situation* of being single, that is maintaining your misery. So if you can address this way of thinking and change it – and work on boosting your own sense of self-responsibility and self-esteem – then everything will improve.

Bridget realised that there were worse things in life than being alone, and that was a big breakthrough for her. Unfortunately, many people never grasp this. For example, I've lost count of the number of women I've known who have been in hopeless, long-term, clandestine affairs and who have told me:

'He made me stay with him. He manipulated my emotions and every time I tried to get out of it, he reeled me back in with compliments and presents. I had no choice but to stick with it – you see, anything's better than being on my own.'

Such women genuinely believe that being alone would be the worst thing in the world. And because they feel that, they develop a very victim-like mentality. In fact, they seem to assume that they have no choices – which is completely barmy.

When we believe that we have no control, and that life as a single person spells utter failure, degradation and misery, we neglect our responsibility to ourselves and we turn ourselves into victims.

Most of us nowadays can expect to have several significant relationships in our lives. This means that between these relationships we are sometimes going to find ourselves single again. It is essential – for your own happiness and self-esteem – that you regard these periods in your life as just as viable as those when you are in a relationship. If you don't, then you will always tend to stay in relationships that aren't very good for you.

There are a lot of ideas in Chapter Seventeen which should encourage you to enjoy your single life. And there is also a lot of information in the Directory at the back of the book which will help you.

But for now, just try to take on board that life is very much happier for a single person than it is for someone 'trapped' in a bad relationship.

Deciding on a Partner – and the Timing of Finding One

When a newspaper or magazine writes about a happily married couple or reports their long-term wedding anniversary, there's usually an account of how the couple met: 'As soon as I saw him, I knew he was the one for me,' they'll say. Or they might even recall: 'I saw her across a crowded room and I thought – that's the woman I'm going to marry.'

I never know if these stories have grown with the telling, or whether the initial conviction was really that great at the time. I suppose it doesn't matter – when everything turns out so well. But – and I'm sorry to sound such an old cynic – I am quite sure that people very frequently decide that someone is the girl for them, or that the guy over there is *the one*, and the final outcome is anything but happy. It's just that we don't read about these cases.

Truly romantic people often believe that love comes out of the blue and turns their life upside down and that there may only be one true love per person. I'm afraid I don't agree. In truth, most of us get into relationships when we feel *ready* to have them. We often fall in love with someone around the time that our closest friends are all starting relationships, or getting engaged or married. We frequently go looking for love when we're finally qualified, or when we've got enough money to buy a house, or when we're desperate to be a parent.

I'm not saying that romance doesn't come into it. Of course it does. But so does timing. Although some people do meet and marry – highly successfully – someone they meet totally by chance, the vast majority of us fall in love with individuals we've known for a while, or work with, or with whom we share similar levels of attractiveness, political views and interests.

In other words, though we make a romantic choice, it's within a range that we've already – consciously or unconsciously – narrowed down.

I get a lot of emails from distressed individuals whose relationships have gone wrong. I also see men and women with relationship breakdowns in my own counselling practice. And the truth is that very often these relationships have been viewed in completely different ways by the two people involved in them.

Frequently, one of the participants has made a decision that *this is the one* – but this decision hasn't been made jointly, or on the basis of superb compatibility. No, it's been made by one person – and usually because that individual has believed that he or she *must* have a committed relationship, because this is the *time* to have one.

I've had countless female clients whose relationships have failed, who've cried: 'But I'm thirty-six, for God's sake. I *can't* start again. I need to have a baby and I was so sure he was the one, and that he'd make a great father. He knew I wanted to get married and start a family. How *could* he let me down? I can't believe he's acted so callously . . .'

Now this kind of situation is very heartbreaking for such a woman. And there is no doubt that she is desperately upset and hurt. But she is usually far more upset that her plans have gone wrong than she is about the man himself.

We all go through life assuming things. And many women quietly assume: 'By the time I'm thirty-five, I'll be married with kids.' It's OK to assume this, but not to believe that it is a rule of the universe. In other words, if a woman would *prefer* that this should happen, that's fine. But if she believes that it absolutely *must* happen, then her belief will encourage very unhealthy and rigid thinking – especially when she hits her mid-thirties.

So when such a woman meets a new guy, she often *decides* that this bloke is going to be her husband and the father of her children – simply because it's time she found someone and she *must* get on with it – even though there's no evidence that the relationship is that serious, or that the man wants these things too.

But men, too, often decide that it's time to make a permanent match: 'I realised I was just so pissed off with living alone,' they'll say. 'I'm tired of being in London and I want to move out to the country and have a wife and two kids and a couple of dogs. That's where I see myself now – and I was really sure that she was the one I'd do it with.'

Again, such individuals feel very upset, and often angry, when their plans go wrong. This is because they have made a decision which, they believe, *must* happen. And they feel hugely cheated when it doesn't.

So, much of the pain at the failure of a relationship is really to do with the stage someone is at, and their personal view of that stage, rather than to do with the loss of the person they had *decided* to wed.

Nowadays, we do tend to think we can organise everything. We decide that we'll go to university, then go travelling for a year, then we'll get a job, and after a few years we'll buy a house, then we'll find the right partner and get married and raise a family. There are even very high-powered women who seem to manage to have their babies to order – for example, they conceive in the spring and have their offspring during the next Christmas break!

There's nothing wrong with planning or structure. But there is something wrong if we feel that our plans *must* happen. The truth is that there's no rule enshrined in the universe that says that because I decide on something, it *must* happen. And there's no rule that says it must happen for you either.

I'll be returning to how you can change this kind of thinking in a moment. But for now, just cast your mind back. Was your past relationship a truly mutual romance, or did you make up your mind about it before it had a chance to develop – simply because the time was right?

The increasingly loud ticking of a biological clock can be deafening, but it doesn't give you the *right* to get what you want when you want it. You can only *hope* to do that. And there's no point railing against the universe if it doesn't happen.

Desperate people do not, by the way, tend to make good partners. They invariably have an air of anxiety about them, which is not very restful to live with. And the object of their love can easily feel that they are being rushed into commitment because of the other person's agenda. They may also get the feeling that if they weren't around, their partner would quickly choose someone else.

Not surprisingly, many such relationships are fraught with tension throughout, so no wonder they don't survive. Moreover, they are often very volatile and really hard work. All relationships need to be worked at, but this type of liaison is frequently far too much like hard work to be enjoyable or normal.

Even when a relationship is promising, it can be ruined by a woman suddenly getting very upset, just three weeks into it, and demanding to know: 'Do you think this romance is going anywhere? I mean, are we going to get married, d'you think? Because I haven't got time to waste!'

Or a man who is desperate to settle down may say something like: 'I want to make this a really special birthday for you, because by next year at this time, I expect you'll be pregnant, so we won't be able to go out clubbing then.' This is fine if his beloved has a similar agenda, but if not, then it can be a bit of a shock to the system.

You may think that these are very extreme examples of what goes on – but I can assure you that they're not.

All this tension over timing is not a good grounding for a happy, equal relationship – which is why so many of them fail.

Perhaps you were in a hurry in your last relationship? Maybe you had that look of desperation that can be so off-putting? Perhaps your sadness now has much to do with your belief that somehow this was the one that should have worked – or even that you've had your last chance. These thoughts are not logical. And they're certainly not helpful – because they're hindering your recovery.

Believing That the Failure of Your Relationship Is Terribly Unfair

Most of us know that life isn't fair. If it were, no one with a bad criminal record would win the lottery! Nor would anyone who had ever abandoned a wife and children, or who was already rich. Instead, the lottery would always be won by some meek, self-sacrificing person who had never asked for anything in her life.

And if life were really fair, there would be no extreme poverty, no dictatorships, no NHS waiting lists and no injustice.

Despite what we know intellectually, however, there are plenty of individuals who seem to believe that life must never be unfair – for *them*. I had a boyfriend once who used to regard a rainy day as a personal insult if he had decided to paint his house, or to go out rambling. He felt the weather was unfair – to *him*. And he would plunge into a seriously depressed mood that might go on for weeks.

This is not normal. When a relationship comes to an end for someone who believes that life must not be unfair to *them*, it is this belief that makes recovering from the break up so difficult.

In contrast, mentally healthy people have a well-developed sense of tolerance. They would, of course, prefer that things go well, but if they don't, they recover from the set-back. They are also good at putting up with discomfort in order to make an improvement. For example, someone who has good mental health, but who is also overweight, understands that you have to put up with temporary discomfort – by not eating things you want to eat – in order to achieve your greater goal of weight loss.

But individuals who have poor mental tolerance keep eating the 'forbidden' foods because they want to eat them, and because they taste nice – and they seem to think there's some sort of universal conspiracy against them because they can't eat all they want and also lose weight. They think life's unfair – but that it *mustn't* be unfair to them.

As you can see, this kind of thinking spells death to any diet! And it also prevents recovery from a broken heart. People who think this way will take a long time to get over the unfairness of the end of their relationship. Some of them *never* get over it.

I've known both men and women who have been so furious that life has been unfair to them in depriving them of their relationships – relationships which, by the way, were often not great – that they have lived like victims, and moaned about their lot till their deaths.

So, even if you think that life has been unfair to you in not allowing you to keep your relationship intact, please try to see that there is no law in the universe that says life must be fair for you. And try to compare this blow – bad though it may be – to the kind of tragedies that many others have to suffer, such as getting cancer, losing a loved one in an act of terrorism, or being born with only half a brain.

Of course, some people don't want to get over the demise of their relationship. They'd far sooner suffer, and ensure that their ex is fully aware of their misery, which ensures that he or she suffers too. But I very much hope that no reader of this book would squander his or her own life and happiness in this way.

All or Nothing

Many people who find life difficult, and who therefore find the end of a relationship very difficult too, think in very polarised ways. They think something is either marvellous or terrible; at work, they may well see themselves either as a brilliant success or a total failure – sometimes on the same day!

These people can often be great fun – because they can be lively and expansive – though their downsides are a bit of a drag, not only for them, but for others close to them.

They often have terrific passions for a particular activity, but when you speak to them about it some time later, you'll frequently find that it has been replaced by some other interest. Psychologists call this sort of thinking 'All or Nothing'.

'All or Nothing' thinking is a real curse in relationships – both when you're in one, and when you're trying to get over one.

Plenty of people reading this book, who opted to get out of a relationship but who can't seem to get over their sadness, will suffer from this syndrome. The type of person who is ecstatically happy one minute but who is cast down if the tiniest thing goes wrong, can find sustaining a relationship very difficult.

Then there are the individuals who adore the feeling of being in love; but as soon as the emotion begins to turn into more normal, authentic, grown-up love and care and belonging, they decide that the magic has gone and that the relationship is untenable.

People who think this way – and the partners of such people – are hurt by this kind of thinking. The men and women who suffer from it frequently fail to make long-term relationships, because no relationship can stay perfect for long enough.

The partners of such people suffer because, having been swept off their feet by huge affirmation and joy and romance, they get dumped very unceremoniously when the initial breathless excitement starts to translate into normal everyday loving.

'All or Nothing' thinking not only ruins many a promising relationship, it can also prevent a good recovery from a past relationship.

People with this type of thinking are often perfectionists. And they will often declare that their previous relationship was so perfect that nothing else will ever match up to it again.

This sounds very romantic, but in fact it's pretty illogical. For a start, a closer look at the relationship is likely to reveal that it wasn't perfect at all – because nothing is! But far worse is the assumption that nothing nice will ever happen romantically again.

As I said at the beginning of this book, we don't have a crystal ball, so we can't possibly know what other relationships could be just around the corner. If you're someone who suffers from All or Nothing thinking, try to start thinking in a more moderate sort of way. Of course, you want things to be great and wonderful, but if you demand that they *must* be fantastic, then you're putting yourself – and those closest to you – through far too much stress because of your unrealistic demands.

All or Nothing thinking can also lead individuals to feel that they had everything – status, financial security, a nice home, happy children and so on – while they were in their relationship, and that losing that relationship leaves them and their lives in ruins. If you think like that, every day will be a struggle and your recovery will be very slow indeed.

Try to modify your way of thinking. Try to see light and shade in things. Try to accept that just because something is not brilliant, it doesn't have to be terrible. And when you hear yourself say something like: 'I was really happy in my marriage, and now my life is total crap', try to examine the 'total crap'.

Is there nothing about your life that is fun, valuable, useful . . . ? Of course there is. So modify your thinking by challenging it, and you will become more mentally healthy. And when you are – you will find a new relationship for all the right reasons.

Rules for Living

We all have some ways of thinking that are distorted – and which therefore cause us distress in certain circumstances. And as we've seen so far in this chapter, these ways of distorted thinking, which can be very ingrained in us, often prevent us recovering from the breakdown of a relationship.

Our own particular way of thinking is unique to each one of us and it influences everything that we do. And the thoughts and beliefs that crop up *most often*, become assumptions. That is to say that we come to *assume* that they are right, and we quote them to ourselves or to others with great authority.

These assumptions, or 'rules for living' as they're often called, often work quite well for us. But they *only* work well when we realise that they are *our* rules and not the rules of the universe. To put it another way, these rules and assumptions of ours are fine if we accept that we cannot guarantee that they will work out as we want. For them to be healthy, we need to accept them as preferences. But if we allow ourselves to think of them as 'must haves', we get into emotional trouble.

These rules or assumptions often take the form of 'if' and 'then' in our minds. For example, 'If I work hard, then I'll get a good grade in my exams.' Believing that if we work hard then there's a good *chance* that we'll do well in our exams is entirely reasonable. It's a good reason for working hard – and if we fail to do well, it will be disappointing, but not the end of the world. This is a healthy way of looking at things. But often when we say: 'If I work hard, then I'll get a good grade in my exams', we mean something rather different. What we actually mean might go something like this: 'If I work hard, then I absolutely *must* get a terrific grade in my exams, and come top of the class, or it will be the end of the world.'

Now, there's a strong possibility that you'll do very well, but there's no guarantee that you will. After all, you may have a lecturer or tutor who doesn't like you marking your paper. Or you may get food poisoning on the day of the exam and under-perform.

If your rule is really rigid – you must do fantastically or it's the end of the world – then you're going to be very disturbed if you achieve anything less than brilliant success. You're also going to go through life very tense and anxious, because this rule of yours – by its very intensity and inflexibility – is going to put you under enormous pressure, and you'll only ever get temporary relief from it when you do extraordinarily well.

So if your rule is rigid and inflexible, life will always be tough for you. And it will be especially difficult if you apply this kind of rule to relationships. If your rule states that if you work hard for something then you must get what you want, but then the love of your life decides that he or she doesn't love you, you're going to be devastated. But it will be your rule, much more than the loss of the actual person, which has caused your devastation.

If someone has a rule which says: 'If I make a decision then it absolutely must be a good one', then he or she is going to feel very cheated and let down if the decision to make someone else their spouse goes wrong. Indeed, they can become seriously hurt and unsettled by being wrong on something so important. I'm not talking at the level of wounded pride here – it's much more painful and serious than that. But of course the truth is that there is no way of guaranteeing that when you make a decision it *must* work out as you planned.

Unfortunately, if you have gone through life believing that when you've decided something, anything at all, it *must* happen, then you are invariably going to be upset when it doesn't.

So our rules for living can cause us so much distress that they delay our recovery from a broken heart.

To come back to you and your relationship, do you have some rules which might be maintaining your misery now? Apart from those already discussed there are plenty of other possibilities, including:

- If I love someone overwhelmingly, then that person must love me back.
- If I put my trust in someone, then that person must be utterly trustworthy in return.
- If I am faithful, then my partner must be faithful too.
- If someone promises to love me for ever, they must keep that promise.
- If I want something badly enough, then I must have it.
- If I am decent and fair and kind, then other people must be equally decent and fair and kind.
- If I make the momentous decision to marry, then it must last for ever.
- If someone loves me, they must be financially generous to me at all times.

Does any of this ring a bell with you? Do you think it is possible that the way you think is maintaining your misery? If it is, then just knowing about it will begin to help you to think in a different way.

But the way we think – and the rules we have – has evolved over our whole lifetime, so it would be unrealistic to believe that we can completely change overnight. However, you *can* change, step by step. Plenty of people do – and their lives are much happier as a result.

Try to spot when your thinking is rigid, unhelpful and unhealthy. And ask yourself what rule is there in the universe that supports how you think? You can also ask yourself what you would think of someone else if he or she had the same thoughts, beliefs and rules. Would you think that person was mentally healthy? Would you think that that person was helping him or herself to have a normal, healthy life – and to succeed in loving relationships? You probably wouldn't. And it's not helping you, either.

So try to stop thinking that:

- other people *make* you think, or feel things;
- you are a lesser person if you're single rather than in a relationship;
- you are a victim of circumstances;
- you have no control;
- it's dreadful that you were let down by someone when you had decided that that person was the love of your life;
- it's dreadful that you were let down by your ex just when you felt that the time was right to have a lasting relationship – and maybe a family;
- life should be fair to you (even though you know that it isn't fair for vast numbers of people round the world);
- if something isn't brilliant, it's terrible;
- your rules and assumptions are always right and that they guarantee you'll get what you want.

Changing your thinking is hard – but if you do it, you'll change your life for the better.

15

Professional Help to Aid Your Recovery

Do You Need It?

Let's face it, heartbreak is part of life – albeit a very sad part. Generally, it should not turn into an illness. The normal response to the ending of a relationship is unhappiness – which can last quite a few months.

As we have already discussed, we need to lean on our friends during this period. We also need to nurture ourselves.

Usually, quite soon after the break-up of a relationship, we throw ourselves into our jobs to take our minds off our home situation. Later, we start socialising again, usually in groups, and then we begin to look forward to the day when we may meet someone special with whom we can have a new relationship.

This is pretty much a normal response to heartbreak. And we tend to look back at our past relationship and say something like: 'OK, I made a few mistakes there, and maybe I was a bit unlucky, and I'm not sure the timing of the whole thing was great, but that's how things go sometimes. Much of it was good.

Some of it was bad. I can learn from it and I can get over it. And just because this has gone wrong, it doesn't mean that I can't have a good relationship in the future. I know the world is full of very nice, decent, loving people – plenty of whom would make good partners.'

But supposing that, several months after the end of your romance, you are still desperately unhappy. What if, despite reading this book, undertaking the recommended tasks, attempting to put the record straight and trying to examine if your own thoughts are responsible for your misery, you feel as heartbroken as you did right at the beginning?

If this is the case, you might want to consider having some sort of therapy, or getting some medication from your GP, or both.

Earlier in the book, I made the point that it was pretty ridiculous to go and get anti-depressants right after the breakdown of a relationship. You're *supposed* to feel sad then. And you need to try to go through the normal process of recovery. You can't expect an instant fix.

But if, as time goes on, you are still very miserable, then an anti-depressant may help. And I believe you really need to see your GP if any of the following apply to you:

- You feel suicidal.
- You have sleep problems – particularly if you can get off to sleep OK, but you always wake up in the early hours of the morning and find it hard to fall asleep again.
- Your job is suffering because you can't concentrate or because you keep taking days off.
- You feel exhausted all the time.
- You can't be bothered to see your friends or ring them up.
- You have continued to cry a lot.

Apart from depressed people, who else should consider some kind of medical help or counselling at this time? I think that many individuals who are taking a while to get over the heartbreak of a failed relationship could benefit from some talking therapy.

If, for example, you feel terribly hurt by rejection – and this pain is not getting better – I do think it would be good to talk about it. If you seem to have had a run of bad relationships and maybe have kept appearing to make the same mistakes – and you feel pretty hopeless about your ability to break this pattern – then therapy would almost certainly help you. If you're feeling tense and irritable and have perhaps started having panic attacks, then I believe you should definitely get some professional help.

And if the last chapter – all about how your negative and irrational thinking can make things worse – has raised various issues for you that you can't resolve alone, then therapy would be a good idea for you too. This is especially true if you have been able to see that you *do* have unhelpful thoughts, but you believe that, in *your* case, it's absolutely impossible to change them. People who need help usually believe that somehow it's always easier for other folk to make changes in their thoughts and behaviour than it is for them!

Let me give you some examples of men and women I've known – either in my practice, or among my friends – who have benefited from seeing a psychotherapist or counsellor.

Zoë

Zoë's marriage ended when her husband had an affair and left her – only one year after they had tied the knot. It had started so well but ended so sadly, and she felt completely demolished by the whole experience.

She had met her husband at work. He was attractive and attentive and he seemed to understand her better than anyone ever had. He surprised her with little treats and outings. And as soon as he got the opportunity, he took her to bed where he turned out to be a brilliant lover. Soon she was experiencing the kind of sex she thought only happened to other people. But the best thing of all was that he adored her. He gave her warmth and love and affirmation – and promised a golden future for them both.

Zoë was completely bowled over by him. Not surprisingly, she fell in love powerfully and passionately. She couldn't believe her luck that this man loved her. And, for the first time in her life, she felt truly alive and really special.

I say 'for the first time' because Zoë came from a family where sex was never mentioned and where her proper, and rather emotionally timid parents, had never given her compliments or even hugged her.

When we get something special from a relationship that seems to be very different from the sort of loving we got as kids, we are overwhelmed by it. We lap it up, like a kitten demolishing a saucer of cream. We can't get enough of it. We cling to it.

This is fine, if it works out, but if it doesn't, we are totally devastated. We are devastated not only because of the loss of the relationship and all that it promised, but because we have opened ourselves up to the complete sort of love and affirmation that we never had. Furthermore, we become panic-stricken at the idea that something we've longed for, and that we've had for such a short time, is going to be taken away.

Unfortunately, that is exactly what happened to Zoë. Shortly after her marriage, she realised that her husband, though charming and attractive, was not very keen on commitment or fidelity – and that he had a very wandering eye.

She became jealous and tried to keep tabs on him. She spied on him at work, and often turned up at the pub or when he played football, just because she was so worried about what he might get up to.

The more unsettled she became, the more he withdrew from her. Despite his lifelong promises of love, he seemed to tire of her now that she was his wife.

And the more he showed his indifference, the more jealous and anxious she became. They started rowing and she lived in a state of panic that he would leave her – which of course, he finally did.

Fortunately, she had the good sense – and the financial capability – to take herself off to a therapist who specialised in relationships. Over the next few months she explored what had gone wrong in her marriage. She also came to understand, for the first time, how very bereft of love she had felt for most of her life – starting from when she was very small.

She felt guilty talking about her parents in a negative way. She used to say to the therapist: 'They weren't awful. They loved me in their own way. They would be appalled if they could hear me now. I'm sure they did their best. I wasn't starved or deprived.'

But gradually she did let herself explore all the times when she had tried to make an effort to please them, and they had been embarrassed by her efforts. She recalled how she would try to hug her parents in public, but how they would push her away and tell her to stop being so over-dramatic. She also remembered how her best friend's mother used to be kind to her and tell her that she looked lovely, whereas her own mother never did.

And the therapist helped her to see that although her parents were not ogres, they had very definitely not been loving *enough*. And that was the point. That was why her great romance had been so important. It had seemed to fill in all the gaps that her emotionally impoverished childhood had left.

Understanding more about herself helped Zoë to put her childhood and her marriage behind her. It also raised her self-esteem, so that she realised that she was entitled to be loved and cherished, and also that she was a worthwhile person.

And a couple of years later, she met someone who thought she was wonderful. The new Zoë was able to accept that she deserved him, which meant that she took the romance much more in her stride. She was more relaxed with him – and she didn't panic every time he was out of her sight.

Zoë has now been happily married for ten years. For her, having some therapy helped her to come to terms with herself, her needs and her own value. And she believes she did herself a great favour by paying to have this counselling. 'It was probably the best thing I ever did for myself, in my life,' she says. 'Even though it was a bit of a financial struggle, and even though it was very painful at the time.'

Kate

Kate – whom you may remember from Chapters 9, 11 and 12 – was dumped by her lecturer lover after seventeen years as his mistress. One of the things that upset her most about losing him was how much she had demeaned herself by staying in the relationship for so long. She found this waste of her time very, very distressing. And she felt that she needed some answers before she could draw a line under such a large segment of her life. She, too, went for some therapy.

During the sessions she had with the female counsellor, she began to understand something she had never seen before. Her lover had been very charismatic and very loving – especially in the early days – but he had also suffered periods of depression, which had always caused great anxiety in Kate.

During therapy, she saw a parallel for the first time between her lover and her mother. Her mother had had several periods of depressive illness when Kate had been young. During those times her mother had, in effect, ceased to be available to her daughter – in fact, she had usually taken to her bed and had become uncommunicative and distant.

Kate recalled how her mother rarely looked at her when she was depressed, and how, as a child, she had felt as if her mother no longer liked or loved her.

'There was no love for me in her eyes,' Kate said to her therapist. 'It was terrifying for me – like the end of the world. I felt a huge sense of panic. And life would be extremely difficult till Mum came out of the depression – when she would always be extra-loving to try to make up for the previous months of her illness.

Through counselling, Kate began to understand how often we look for someone who is similar to our parents – but someone who is a more perfect version of them. And how we can feel terrified if they turn out to have the same flaws that our parents had – flaws that upset us so much when we were children, but which affect us even more powerfully when we experience them again as adults.

Kate got some low-cost counselling through a professional organisation who operated a reduced charge for clients willing to be counselled by trainee therapists. This worked very well for her. Her therapist was young and keen – and was supervised by an older psychotherapist who had enormous experience. Also, her therapy was affordable.

Therapy helped Kate to see some of the reasons why she had hung on in there with her lover. And having revisited the problems that had made her feel insecure and unwanted as a child, she began to see that these problems need not hold her back any more.

Tom

Tom left his wife, Lynne, after twenty-five years of marriage. He knew he had done the right thing. In fact, he had been planning to leave for years – but had not gone until his son and daughter had left home. So there was nothing sudden about his decision.

But he did feel guilty, and his guilt weighed so heavily on him that he became depressed. So he went to see his GP. The doctor was sympathetic and said he was prepared to prescribe some anti-depressants. Tom wasn't very keen on this, so the doctor suggested he should go and see a relationships counsellor.

Tom opted to go to Relate. He saw a woman counsellor and was, at first, very wary of opening up to her as he felt that she would automatically take his ex-wife's side. This didn't happen and he spent three sessions talking about what makes relationships work, what's normal, what one can expect from a normal marriage, and so on.

After the three sessions, he felt that he had come to terms with what he had done. He also understood that it takes two to make a marriage, and he was able to acknowledge that he had felt lonely and disappointed in his relationship – and that having hung on in there for twenty-five years, he really had little to feel guilty about.

The sessions did not act like a magic wand on his mood, but he felt more equipped to deal with his situation and to get on with making a new life.

Maria

Maria was married for thirty years. It had never occurred to her to question how good or how bad her marriage was. No one in her family had ever been divorced and she came from the sort of family – and from the sort of time – where girls were not expected to have any career other than that of being a wife and mother.

When her husband walked out on her, she was totally shocked – and she simply could not recover from the anxiety that now pervaded her every thought. She felt vulnerable in a way that she had never felt in her life – and being a stoical woman who believed that 'you just have to get on with whatever life throws at you', she was appalled at herself for becoming a 'nervous wreck'.

She was in fact so nervy and upset that she developed agoraphobia, and she began to think that her useful life was at an end.

Fortunately, Maria had an excellent GP who had a counsellor attached to his practice. Maria felt unable to go to the surgery, because of her fear of going out, but she had phone-counselling – which helped a bit.

Then a friend suggested that she ring a support group called the National Phobics Society. This turned out to be her best move. She found them to be very helpful and non-judgemental, and she began to see that what had happened to her was understandable and not simply weakness.

It was a good six months before Maria started to feel anything like her old self. But she credits the National Phobics Society with turning her life around.

Where to Get Free or Low-Cost Help

If you want free professional help in the UK, then you need to start with your own doctor. Most GPs are sympathetic, kind people, but usually they are also very busy ones, with their own stresses and strains.

To get the best out of your visit to the surgery, I suggest that you try to book a double appointment. Assuming your doctor allocates ten minutes per patient, this should give you almost twenty minutes to talk – and will give your doctor time to listen. But check how long your GP's appointments are when you ring up the receptionist.

The vast majority of GPs will consider putting a depressed patient on anti-depressants – and they should explain how long these pills will take to work, and what the possible side-effects might be.

But not everyone who is depressed after the break-up of a relationship wants to have medication. Plenty of people in this situation feel that they know very well *why* they are depressed. What they really want is to talk it out, to try to examine why the relationship went wrong, and to tell someone about their sense of injustice about the whole thing.

I sympathise with this view, but if you are suffering badly, I do think that sometimes a bit of chemical help can elevate you to a point where counselling will be more effective. It's difficult to generalise, however, and you will really have to be guided by your own doctor.

Some GP practices have a counsellor attached to them. If your practice is one of those, and if the GP recommends you for counselling, I should take up the offer. Usually you will be given six sessions, free of charge, and the chances are that this will help you – not just in the present difficult circumstances, but for life.

You might notice, however, that I say 'the chances are that this will help you'. I say this because not all counsellors suit all patients. That's a fact of life. Even the most experienced and highly qualified therapist will fail to help some people.

Normally, if you were paying for the service, I would say, move on to someone you feel more at home with. But in this particular situation, where you're being treated on the NHS, my advice would be to stick it out. You'll almost certainly learn something over the six sessions, and should feel better simply for having a professional sit and listen to you, even if the therapeutic relationship is not made in heaven!

What about tranquillisers? Obviously many individuals do suffer severe anxiety when they are emerging from a broken relationship.

In the past, many doctors would have prescribed a tranquilliser. Some doctors may still do – particularly for someone whose partner has suddenly died, or walked out. But all responsible doctors now accept that tranquillisers are extremely addictive and that they should only be prescribed for a very short time. So, your GP will almost certainly be reluctant to prescribe them for you in the aftermath of your relationship split.

But if you are extremely anxious or depressed, might your GP refer you on to an NHS specialist? Much depends on what the mental health provision is like in your area. If you are profoundly depressed, or anxious or phobic, your doctor may suggest referring you to a psychiatrist, or a clinical psychologist. But it is unlikely that you'll be seen by anyone very quickly.

While we're on the subject of the NHS, I must mention that some people who are recovering from a broken relationship have very real problems with sex. Some women, for example, have difficulty with intercourse – they may fear penetration, or actively dislike it for some other reason. Some men whose relationships have gone awry have sex problems too. The most common ones are Erectile Dysfunction (or Impotence), Premature Ejaculation (coming too quickly), and Retarded Ejaculation – which is also known as Ejaculatory Incompetence (inability to ejaculate easily).

There is some free help for all these problems, but again, much depends upon the area you live in. Family Planning Clinics do offer some psychosexual counselling. And there are psychosexual units within the NHS up and down the country. But some areas are well-served with this kind of help, while others have very little on offer – which means that there are always very long waiting lists.

So, moving on from the NHS, what else is available? Support groups do a great job in this country. Organisations such as The Depression Alliance, for people with depression, and the National Phobics Society, for people with anxiety and phobias, have helped countless individuals. Getting support from lay people who have experienced what you're going through can be a tremendous help. These organisations usually have a helpline and a website – and you'll also be offered a lot of printed leaflets containing much relevant information.

Many distressed people find that help from a support group – often supplemented by reading appropriate self-help books – is all that is needed to help them through this difficult time of their lives.

There are organisations that help with sexual problems, with depression, with panic attacks, and with anxiety and phobias. Precise details for these are available at the back of this book in the Help Yourself Directory.

Support groups often offer free, or very low-cost help. Then there are agencies who actually provide one-to-one low-cost therapy.

If you want to put your past relationship into some sort of context and look at what went wrong in a bid to understand things better and to try to ensure that you don't repeat your mistakes, then in my view, your best bet would be Relate.

Relate, which used to be called Marriage Guidance, sees couples or individuals of any sexual orientation who are experiencing difficulties connected with relationships. They operate in England, Wales and Northern Ireland.

Nowadays, you can get a great deal of help simply by visiting their website – because apart from offering traditional face-to-face counselling, Relate now also provide an email service, online counselling and phone counselling.

Some Relate counsellors are also trained as psychosexual therapists.

Relate's charges are assessed according to your income, but whatever you earn, they are likely to be less than the fees levied in the private sector.

Scotland is not covered by Relate. Instead there is Couples Counselling Scotland, an equally good agency.

For readers who are under twenty-five, there are also Brook Advisory Centres. Their main purpose is to counsel on sex and contraception, but the doctors at Brook – who are almost all women – are very experienced in relationship matters.

Also for those under twenty-five, there is an umbrella organisation called Youth Access, which has drop-in counselling centres nationwide. These centres all have their own local names, but you can contact Youth Access and ask what provision there is in your area.

Private Therapy

If you decide to have some private therapy or counselling, you have masses of options to choose from, but this choice can be quite bewildering.

In my previous Help Yourself book, *Get the Self-Esteem Habit,* I did attempt to explain in some detail just what is available in the private sector.

Alas, I don't have the space to go into all of this again in *this* book, but I will give you an abbreviated run-down of what's on offer – and also try to answer the most frequently asked questions in the next few pages.

Types of Therapist

There are basically four different kinds of talking therapist: psychiatrists, psychologists, psychotherapists and counsellors.

- Psychiatrists are medical doctors who have specialised in mental health. They are not all trained in talking to patients or counselling them – especially those who work exclusively in the NHS: some of those are much more interested in what medication can achieve. But those psychiatrists who have private practices will almost all have good talking therapy skills. And the advantage of seeing a psychiatrist is that – because he's a doctor – if you need time off work he can sign a sick note for you, and he can of course also prescribe medication should you need it.
- Psychologists are not medical doctors. And they aren't necessarily qualified in talking therapies either. Many of them are academics who never treat patients at all. If you want to see a psychologist for help with your problems, you need to go looking for a clinical psychologist, or a chartered psychologist.
- Psychotherapists and counsellors: there used to be a

difference between psychotherapists and counsellors – but nowadays there really is not. For example, I usually call myself a psychotherapist, but someone with identical qualifications to mine might call herself a counsellor. So, some practitioners call themselves one thing, some another. Both psychotherapists and counsellors have been trained in talking to people and in helping them resolve their problems.

At the present time, there is no legal regulation of such individuals. In other words, anyone can put a brass plate up outside their front door and start treating people. So when you're considering who to go to, it is wise to pick someone who is registered or accredited with one of the professional organisations listed in the Directory at the back of the book.

All these organisations require their members to have professional training and experience – and to have professional insurance.

However, I think it's only fair to say that someone with a string of qualifications who's been treating people for years may not necessarily suit you, whereas someone newly qualified may. Finding the right therapist is quite a subjective thing, and the most important point I can make is that – so long as the person has adequate training – you should select someone with whom you feel comfortable.

I know some really wonderful practitioners who do marvellous work with patients. But frankly, I also know of at least two highly regarded mental health and counselling specialists whose own attitudes seem to me to be so totally dysfunctional that I wouldn't send a dog to either of them!

So don't feel that you can't get a good therapist unless they're in Harley Street and are tremendously well known, or expensive. There are masses of unsung heroes: practitioners who will never hit the headlines but who are properly trained, insightful, sympathetic, inspirational people doing a great job with and for their patients.

Types of Therapy

There are countless types of therapy. But, as someone coming to terms with the end of a relationship, the chances are that you're going to be looking for a therapist who's got a lot of experience in sex and relationship matters. So your first port of call might well be the British Association for Sexual and Relationship Therapists (BASRT). Their counsellors specialise in relationship matters and could well be of the most use to you in finding out what went wrong in your past and what you can put right for the future.

If you have responded well to the material in this book about how our thoughts influence our moods and how our view of things – rather than the things themselves – cause us trouble, then you will probably do very well with someone who specialises in cognitive therapy or cognitive behaviour therapy.

If you want to delve into your early years, you may prefer a therapist with a more analytical approach. Such practitioners usually call themselves psychodynamic therapists and include adherents to the work of Freud and Jung.

This kind of therapy is likely to be long-term – so don't consider it if you want short-term therapy or if you cannot commit to therapy at least once a week for quite a long period of time. To benefit from psychodynamic therapy you need to be able to find substantial money and time.

There are also vast numbers of counsellors who consider themselves to be 'integrative' or 'eclectic' in their approach. This simply means that they don't adhere strictly to any one school of thought but will tailor treatment according to the needs of the client.

Finally, let me briefly mention hypnosis. Personally, I don't think that hypnosis is a good idea for depressed people. Neither do I think it helps very much when it comes to examining exactly what has gone wrong with your relationship.

However, hypnosis is very valuable when it comes to healing feelings of hurt. It can also help with self-esteem issues. And, in my opinion, it is one of the best forms of therapy when looking to help anxiety and stress. Most hypnotherapists can help you to relax – and most clients love this aspect of the process. Many therapists will teach self-hypnosis to their clients – and I believe that regular self-hypnosis is a very powerful tool that anyone can use in helping himself or herself to feel calmer and more capable.

Whatever kind of therapy you fancy, it is much easier today than it used to be to pick a therapist, as most of the main counselling/therapeutic organisations have websites. There are also whole books devoted to different types of therapy.

My advice is to take your time, do your homework, and go with what feels likely to be most useful for you.

Many individuals ask their friends for their recommendations – and often choose a therapist because someone they know has seen this person. This can work out very well – but it doesn't always. I've known instances where a counsellor was wonderful for one person, but wasn't able to help her friend. There is absolutely no guarantee that a therapist who suited a pal of yours will necessarily suit you.

The whole process of good therapy is very collaborative. And the mixture of the two personalities involved (the client and the therapist) is, in my view, key to the eventual success. It's rather like a marriage – but without sex!

Frequently Asked Questions

Q: *If I have therapy, how soon will I feel better?*
A: I have no idea! And no therapist can give any real guarantees. Most adults leave their first counselling session feeling better for having got a lot of stuff off their chests. Some people feel markedly improved for having just a couple of sessions with a relationships counsellor. Others may go to about twelve sessions with a cognitive or cognitive-behaviour therapist and might well find that they learn lessons from

that therapy that help them for the rest of their lives. Yet others may embark on at least two years of therapy with an analytical practitioner and swear that it is the best thing they've ever done for themselves. Meanwhile, other similar people may be disappointed in therapy, and will leave the process. And some individuals begin seeing a counsellor for some short-term therapy, but discover that they have so many problems that they continue having therapy for years.

Q: *How much will it cost?*
A: You may get counselling in some parts of the country for as little as £25 per hour. (Relate's costs – as I've mentioned earlier in this section – are often lower than this.) Some people – like Kate, whom I talked about earlier in this chapter – take advantage of low-cost counselling which is available through some of the professional organisations as part of their training of their own therapists. Most people can find some sort of therapy at around £30–£40 per hour. But prices can vary hugely depending upon where you are in the country. And if you want to see a top psychiatrist – in Harley Street, for example – you could easily be talking about well over £100 per session.

Q: *How will I know if the therapist is experienced in my problems?*
A: Before seeing any therapist you should ring or email him or her. And you should expect to get good, clear answers to any reasonable questions. So, ask what experience the therapist has with your problems. Ask, too, what sort of approach he or she is likely to take.

Q: *What will happen if I can't afford to see the therapist regularly?*
A: Many counsellors or therapists will agree to see people fortnightly, or even at three-week intervals if cost is a problem. But some therapists – those of an analytical nature in

particular – insist on more regular attendance. This is another thing you need to ask before you select a therapist. You also need to bear in mind that many therapists are paying out rent on their consulting rooms, and will charge you for missed appointments if you cancel with less than forty-eight hours' notice.

Finally, before you start searching for a counsellor, do have a look at the Help Yourself Directory at the end of this book where I have listed details of a number of good professional therapeutic organisations. I would advise you to select your therapist from one of these.

16

Accentuating the Positive

After a break-up, it can be very hard to enjoy our single lives, or to form new romantic liaisons, unless we can see and acknowledge some good in our *past* relationship.

Right at the beginning of the book, I discussed the feelings of grief and bereavement associated with a broken love affair and compared them with the feelings one gets when a partner dies. There are very many similarities between the two situations – and perhaps as you've worked through this book so far, you have been struck by just how many you have found.

But the major difference between the end of a relationship and someone dying, is that death brings with it certain rituals – a funeral, a death certificate, the organising of a burial plot, or a decision about scattering your loved one's ashes. The British – the English in particular – keep these rituals to a minimum. But even so, they serve to draw a line under one chapter of our lives.

However, the end of a relationship can pass almost unnoticed. Even a divorce nowadays rarely involves any attendance in court. And for someone who has loved deeply, but has not married, or not had children, it can sometimes seem as though the past relationship is so quickly forgotten by everyone else that it begins to appear like a dream.

In Chapter Thirteen, I mentioned some methods that people use to set the record straight and enable themselves to move on – such as writing an account of the relationship and then burning it. But many readers will not have indulged in any kind of ceremony at this point. And those who have may well have been concentrating on everything that was *bad*.

So now, at the end of this second section of the book, I want you to consider finding some value in your past relationship – no matter how difficult or destructive it may have been – and to find some way of celebrating or commemorating that value.

My reason for suggesting this is that all too often people want to go on and have fresh relationships – but their hearts are still full of bitterness concerning their last one. In truth, bitterness rarely damages the person you feel bitter *about*: mostly it damages *you*.

Including this idea in the book has, to be frank, caused me to rethink my own previous relationships – as I never ask anyone to do something I haven't done, or am not prepared to do myself. I have reviewed my feelings about the three significant relationships which I had as an adult prior to meeting my husband.

I found that, with two of them, I was able to see many good points and to recall them with some pleasure – despite the fact that they were both rather difficult partnerships that caused me a lot of pain. But I was able to evaluate the good that each relationship did me – and I think that was a helpful thing to do.

One of these men gave me a great deal of affirmation and confidence in my work. He was also good fun to be with and he introduced me to a level of sophistication – in eating, drinking and so on – that was previously unknown to me, and seemed important at the time! Furthermore, his attraction to me provided a very welcome boost to my belief in myself as a woman at that time.

The other guy loved me very powerfully and romantically. And though our relationship did not work out, I remember him with great fondness and gratitude.

But my stumbling block comes with the other man, whom I'll call Mark.

In truth, although it was a long time ago, I find it very hard to recall anything good about my relationship with Mark. I have tried – but nothing comes to mind. My bid to find value in that relationship was pretty fruitless. And then I realised what I had to do. I had to forgive *myself* for getting into it and putting up with it.

I realise now that for a very long time, whenever I have thought of Mark, I have felt extraordinarily angry. And I have now pinned down what that anger was about. It was anger at myself, for allowing myself to waste so much time, for putting up with such lousy sex, for enduring endless, unjustifiable moods, tantrums, and non-communication, and for thinking that I was trapped and could do nothing about my misery.

This all seems like weakness now.

But in my desire to find something good about the relationship, I've come to the realisation that what was holding me back in drawing a line under it – although it was a very long time ago – was my fury at myself. So I have forgiven myself and to commemorate that forgiveness, I am planning to treat myself to a whole series of CDs that I've wanted for a long time!

That relationship was *then*. I acknowledge that I did what I thought was right at the time, and that this does not mean that I was weak, hopeless or stupid. It simply means that I did not know what I know now. That is how I have come to view these past relationships. And my journey to find the good in them has given me more peace of mind.

So, what about *your* past relationship – the one that prompted the purchase of this book? Can you easily find good things about it – like I could with two of my past lovers? Or is it a tough call – like my problems with Mark?

I believe that you will be able to find something good – no matter how small – about that person, or about what has happened to you, or about the experience that you have gained from the relationship.

Once you have found it, I think it would be a good idea for you to acknowledge this good discovery in some way.

You may want to send a thank-you card to your former lover – expressing gratitude for the positive aspects of your relationship. You may want to plant a tree, or a window box, as a lasting token of a love that promised much – and had its good points – though it failed to last. You may decide to make some sort of charity donation. Or you may choose to do something more creative. One of my clients was a musician, and she wrote a piece of music in memory of the friendship that she valued within a flawed relationship.

And if you need to forgive yourself for the past, then it would be a good idea to treat yourself to something that is a bit of an extravagance – something that will last and will remind you that you're a survivor.

'The past is a foreign country: they do things differently there,' wrote L.P. Hartley in *The Go-Between*. And that is true. You're not going back there. But it's important that you don't hate it – and that you don't regret that you ever went.

Part Three

Starting Again

17

Embracing Your Single Life

You may well read this chapter – or at least dip into it – quite early on, when you are still seriously heartbroken. But let me just say that you won't be ready to deal with all this information at that stage.

Much of the advice contained here is really only suitable for those individuals who have not only worked their way through the first two sections of the book, but who have also been on their own for several months.

I've talked a lot already about my belief that you should regard yourself as an independent person in life – no matter whether you are in a relationship or not – and that you should, as a consequence, take responsibility for your own development, social life and happiness at all times.

I have also tried to imbue you with the idea that being without a partner is something that is going to happen to us all several times in our lifetimes – if we're lucky enough to live to old age.

I have done my best to suggest to you that being single is not a time for mentally 'treading water' till you're allowed back into the glorified world of couples! And also that single people should perceive themselves to be just as special as any one who happens to be in a relationship.

Now, I am aware that some readers will know that I am in a second marriage – which is a very happy one. And I do suspect therefore that you may read what I think and believe, and then say to yourself: 'Well, it's OK for her to have these views – but then, she's not on her own.'

I think this is understandable. After all, I'm not having to live as a single person. But – and this is the important point – I *have* done so. I have very clear memories of being on my own for five years between marriages.

Moreover, I see other people – patients, friends and relatives – going from single status to being part of a couple then back to being single again. And all I can say is that this is now *normal*, and the important thing is to value yourself – for all that you are, and can contribute – every day of your life.

So in this chapter, I want to concentrate on things you can do to make your single life fulfilling, fun and active.

Exploring Your Own Company

I remember when I first went to the theatre on my own. I felt really awkward and uneasy, and I was sure that the other theatre-goers were looking at me and wondering why I was so unpopular that I couldn't find anyone to accompany me!

But as the evening wore on, I began to really enjoy it. First of all, I had the whole interval to myself to read all the interesting notes and articles in the programme, which I could never usually get round to before. Then I began to realise that I didn't have to worry whether any companion was as entranced with the production as I was, which meant that I could relax, as I only had me to please.

That was twenty years ago. And though I have little reason

to go on my own to the cinema or to the theatre these days, I do sometimes still do it. And I really enjoy it.

I also recall going abroad on my own for the first time – when I took myself off to Vienna for a five-day break.

Again, I had moments of trepidation about this trip – mostly about managing the money and the language. But I got on well and felt really pleased with myself as a result. I managed to buy tickets for a concert and an opera while I was there – and I went to both and thoroughly enjoyed them. I also visited several houses – now museums – where famous people had once lived, including Mozart, Beethoven and Freud. In fact, I even ended up sitting on Freud's loo – but that's another story!

The point of mentioning all this is to encourage you to try some solo activities yourself. All too often we don't do things we want to do because we keep waiting for some friend or other to agree to come along on a trip with us – and it never happens. And sometimes these activities don't happen because our friends don't enjoy the same things as us. At the time I went to Vienna, for example, none of my close friends would have been very enthusiastic about what I did there. So, had I not gone alone, I might never have gone at all. And if I had persuaded someone to come with me who had disliked my ideas of how to spend the time, I wouldn't have ended up doing and enjoying the stuff that I did do.

Going alone was frightening. But it worked out fine. And the trip did wonders for my confidence. In fact now, in the twenty-first century, single living has become positively trendy. And therefore it has become much more acceptable to enjoy your own activities, time and space than it was when I was doing it in the early eighties.

There are three times as many people living alone now as there were thirty years ago. And 31 per cent of households in the UK consist of just one person.

This trend has altered our perceptions of people who live alone. We realise that there are choices now, and that there is no longer any stigma to being single.

So if you've never done things on your own – such as going to the cinema, theatre, ice skating, concerts, restaurants and so on – now's the time to try it.

You may not enjoy such occasions as much as you do when you share them with a partner, or with friends – but you might. Plenty of people do. And it's quite liberating to be on your own. You find out more about yourself that way. And being single – no matter how long it lasts – presents an ideal opportunity to try activities or new interests that you've always meant to get round to.

So try enjoying some of your leisure time alone. But don't get too solitary. You need to strike a balance – and one way of doing that is to join an organisation for single people.

Single Living

Single Living, formerly Single Again, is an organisation that encourages its members to celebrate their single lives. In my view, its philosophy is exactly right for our times. It's not a dating agency, though people have met new partners through it, it's a support organisation, and social and friendship club, and it now has a travel company too.

Single Again began in around 1990. And I have been very enthusiastic about its concept from day one.

I think you should know that nowadays I do sometimes get clients from it, and I do get paid for articles I write for its website, so you could say that my interest is not without bias! But I was involved with it long before any money came my way, for the simple reason that it performs a huge service to all single people. And if you want to make a start in changing your life and meeting new adults, I believe that you can't do better than to start with them.

Other Organisations for Singles

If you happen to be in the eighteen to thirty-five age range – male or female – another organisation that might interest you is the National Federation of 18 Plus Groups. This is a non-religious, non-political, activities-based association with fifty groups throughout the UK.

It is not a support group as such, but if the end of your relationship has left you with time on your hands, and you've lost some friends because of the split, then 18 Plus could get you involved in all sorts of activities, and give you the opportunity to meet loads of new people.

There are other organisations up and down the country for divorced, separated and single adults. A good place to find out more is the National Association for the Divorced and Separated.

New Plans

Earlier in the book, I advised readers not to make life-changing alterations such as moving house, relocating to the other end of the country, or abroad, or going travelling. But once you've been alone for around six months, it can be wonderfully exciting to plan to do something entirely different. After all, this time last year you may well have believed that you were in your relationship for life. Now you know differently – and you're alone. So while you've had to make certain changes, or have had changes thrust upon you, it could well be advantageous to make others.

For instance, if you've always wanted to make your living another way, now would be a good time to find out more about it. You can get advice from your local job centre. Or you can find out more about further education from your local authority, or from the Department for Education and Skills website.

Additionally, you could consult one of the many firms or organisations who would put you through some tests to see where your natural aptitudes lie. These assessment processes used to be classed as Vocational Guidance, but nowadays they are more commonly listed in Yellow Pages under Career Advice, or on the Internet as Career Analysis, or Career Counselling.

A change in what you do for a living may well encourage a change of location too. But even if you stay with your current job, you may well feel that the time has come to move house. Much depends on how the demise of your relationship has left your social life.

For some people, the network of friends and contacts they have where they live is their lifeline. Clearly for such individuals a move – especially out of the area – would be crazy. Others feel that, despite their best intentions, they have been unable to completely sever the connection with their old partner and that constantly bumping into him or her, or socialising in a group that has too many memories of that relationship, is holding them back.

Currently, I have two clients who provide good examples of both situations.

Nina broke up with her man after a five-year relationship. It was her choice to end it but, nonetheless, she was quite heart-broken over the way it had failed to work out.

Nina had a joint mortgage with her partner and they co-owned a very pretty flat in West London.

'It's kind of like a village there,' Nina told me. 'It's near the river. There are loads of restaurants. I can get to work easily. I can park there. And many of my friends live nearby.'

Nina and her man had never managed to make very many mutual friends. So she did not have the difficulty experienced by so many people emerging from a relationship, which is that you lose not only your partner, but also a substantial part of your social network too.

And although Nina knew that the flat would have memories

that would be tough to live with, she had always been keener on the apartment than her man had, and she regarded it as a safe haven. Buying-out her boyfriend's share of the flat took all her savings, and a loan from her bank, but she achieved her aim – and though it was a struggle, it gave her a great sense of achievement and some continuity at a time when everything else seemed to be falling apart.

'It would have been different, I think, if we'd jointly made friends with the other couples in our building. But my ex was a very quiet and rather unsociable bloke – so I knew them all, but he didn't,' she said.

For Nina, then, the best option was for her to stay in the job she loved and to remain in touch with her own very supportive network of friends, and also to continue to live in the flat that she adored – even though it was initially a financial struggle.

Sharon's situation was quite different.

Sharon is a quiet person who does not have much self-belief. Her ex-partner was a real 'life and soul of the party' type and Sharon felt that her social life was dramatically improved through knowing him. She also felt more interesting when she was with him.

So, when the relationship ended, her already poor regard for herself took a further knock. Worse than this, all the people she'd socialised with over the past six years were really her partner's friends, and she felt they would not want to know her after the split.

As a result of these fears, when her ex suggested that they stay good friends – even though he'd taken up with a woman who lived locally – Sharon agreed. Sharon's decision breaks one of the basic rules in this book – but of course she hadn't read it then!

Sharon was a member of her market town's amateur dramatic society – and she was talented too – but her ex also belonged to it. Moreover, it wasn't long before he brought along his new lady.

Sharon was also a member of the local squash club. But so was her former love. And so, unfortunately, was his new partner.

Sharon's other main interest was politics and she was a member of the local Liberal Democrats. But guess what? So was her ex.

The only part of her life that Sharon could truly call her own was her flat – as they had never actually lived together. Unfortunately, her ex lived just around the corner. She was fully aware that he had moved in his new lover – in fact, she could hardly leave her own place without tripping over them.

So, for Sharon, it was really essential that she moved house.

At first, however, she was reluctant to go. 'Why should I?' she asked me rather forlornly. But the reason was that she couldn't get over her past relationship because she was geographically and socially just too close to her ex.

It wasn't easy to make changes. But she did it step by step. She went further afield to play squash – and began to enjoy it for the first time in ages.

'I've started playing better,' she told me. 'Because I'm not looking over my shoulder all the time, wondering if my ex and his new girlfriend are about to turn up.'

She started socialising with friends from her office. She took to getting away at weekends and driving around nearby towns to see if she would enjoy living there – and whether she could afford to do so.

Eventually she moved about twenty miles away – to a place that was a commutable distance from her work. She joined another amateur dramatic society and she took up a new interest – learning French at a local evening class – which had nothing whatever to do with her ex.

Of course it wasn't easy to make a whole new circle of friends, but she did it. She also worked on building up better self-esteem so that she could feel that she was a worthwhile person in her own right.

At the moment, Sharon has not yet found a long-term

partner, but she has embraced her single life and is actively enjoying it. And when people do that, it isn't usually very long before they attract a new love – for all the right reasons rather than the wrong ones.

Changing your job, or career, embarking on further education, or making a house move – whether it's a few miles away or to the other end of the country or abroad – are all things that many of us dream about. As I said earlier, it is not a good idea to make drastic changes right after your heartbreak, but once you've been on your own for a while, they can be very beneficial.

Indeed, some individuals make completely different plans from those they might have envisaged had they remained in their relationships, as did Rosemary and Cathy.

Rosemary, a general practitioner, took a sabbatical from her busy practice and went off – courtesy of Voluntary Service Overseas – to be a doctor in the Third World for a year.

It didn't change her life for ever, in that she came back after her year's stint and went back into her old job. But it changed her perspective on all manner of things – which she found extremely therapeutic.

After Cathy's relationship founded, she gave up her job in the City of London and moved back to Ireland, where she had lived as a child. She discovered that she felt she truly belonged there – and now she has a job in the Irish parliament. But she acknowledges that had her boyfriend not walked out on her she might never have returned to her homeland – even though now she can't imagine being anywhere else.

Wherever you move to, you should enjoy the adventure of furnishing and decorating your new place to your personal taste.

When I got out of my first marriage, I rented a cottage until I got myself straight. I remember how I really enjoyed turning this cottage into my home. I can still recall the thrill of putting up pictures – just where *I* wanted them to be. I also remember the joy of arranging all my books and records – and suddenly feeling that I had somewhere to be, that felt personal and safe.

Some people emerging from a relationship have never actually had their own place before. Maybe they used to share a flat with a whole bunch of friends and then they went into their cohabiting situation. So living on your own – even if it's just in a tiny bedsit or studio – can feel exciting and as if this new start isn't such a bad thing after all.

Even if you don't move, this is a good time to make-over your home so that it reflects *your* personality rather than that of your ex partner. Redoing the bedroom in particular can help you reinforce your singleness in a very positive way.

And that's the vital thing at this stage. You are single now – and probably still a bit bemused at everything that has happened to you. But do remember that singleness is not a stigma: it's an opportunity. So get planning for your single life now, and put those plans into practice.

Obviously, if you have children living with you, you have more constraints on what you can do – but everyone can make some changes in how they live, where they live, and in what they do. And there's probably never been a better time than now to make them.

Evening and Weekend Activities

Even if you don't want to make substantial changes in terms of career or location, this is a very good time to extend your brain and your social circle by doing a class or two in something you've always meant to tackle, but somehow never have. Or by returning to some activity that you always loved but shelved because of being busy, or even because your previous partner didn't enjoy it too.

For local classes, your council's education department should be able to help you. Public libraries are also a very good source of information about further education and evening classes, whether for fun or to change your career path. And probably the very best place to see a huge range of courses in every kind of learning imaginable is Learn Direct.

Dance classes are great for lifting the mood and improving the body and also for helping you to meet more like-minded individuals.

Because of the Internet, you can always find someone somewhere offering classes in every kind of dance imaginable. Certainly tap, ballet, jazz, line dancing, salsa, tango, jive, or Scottish or Irish dancing should pose no problems at all.

If art is your thing, there are art classes in abundance throughout the UK. There are also art appreciation weekends. And wherever you live, you will almost certainly be relatively near an art gallery or a museum. Plenty of individuals find that spending a Sunday afternoon looking at paintings is a very soothing yet stimulating way to spend the time. And the opportunity is always there to meet others who enjoy the same things that you do.

If you're a classical music lover, there are evening classes in opera – performing and theory – and in music appreciation. There are orchestras or bands you can join if you're an instrumentalist. There are 'Friends' organisations of virtually every professional orchestra and opera company. And in almost every town in the land there are amateur music societies that stage productions.

Theatre lovers are similarly well-served in terms of education, amateur dramatic societies, and associations that support professional theatres.

As for sport, no one who is even remotely into physical activity should ever be stuck for inspiration. The UK is packed with athletics, tennis, cricket, rugby and football clubs – and even if you don't want to be actively sporty yourself, there's always a need for others to keep the books, make the teas and so on.

Charities, too, are always in need of people to work in their shops, to drive cars, or help in other ways.

Book Groups have become very popular among people who love to read; they are a good way to encourage your reading of material that you might never otherwise get round to, and an excellent way to make new friends. I can't promise that you'll encounter the seething passions and colourful characters that we see in Channel 4's series, *The Book Group*, but that may be no bad thing!

Many men and women have always wanted to speak a foreign language better than they do. There are language classes all over the UK. And if you're lucky enough to live in a university town, you'll probably find that there are classes at the university – usually in the evenings – that will really stretch you.

Or you might want to get into something rather more serious. Recent world events have turned formerly apolitical people – who rarely bothered to vote – into highly political animals. So, maybe now's the time to get involved in a party or group of your choice. You might even consider standing for council elections, or making plans to get yourself into the Westminster, Scottish, Welsh or European parliaments.

Then there's the great outdoors: gardening is a major hobby in this country and you'll have no difficulty in finding a local horticulture society to join.

And one of the best activities I know of for single people is walking. The good old Ramblers Association is a great place to start. If you join them, you'll get fit, never be at a loose end at weekends, and make new friends into the bargain.

Frankly, whatever your interests, there is no excuse for sitting at home, dreaming about getting off your backside and joining something *one* day. Now *is* that day.

Holidays

Earlier, I spoke about the liberation of taking yourself off on holiday alone.

But nowadays, with more single people around (who have money to spend) than at any time in history, travel companies have woken up to the fact that single holiday-makers are huge business. And there is a proliferation of firms specialising in creating trips with single people in mind.

Here are some suggestions of apparently reputable companies in the single's market. I should just say, however, that I haven't personally travelled with any of them, so please don't take their inclusion here as a firm recommendation.

A good first option is to see what Travel Companions has to offer. This is the company that operates under the umbrella of the support organisation Single Living. Travel Companions offers a matching service where they will pair single travellers who have shared interests. Also on the Single Living site, you'll find all sorts of hints and tips about travelling as a single person.

Sovereign Holidays have an offshoot called Small World, which specialises in holidays for lone travellers.

Acorn Activities, though not exclusively for singles, is an organisation that has holidays for everyone – you can do anything from caving and abseiling to painting or furniture restoration.

Other useful companies to know about are Solitaire, Solo Holidays, Friendship Travel, and a new, quite small company called Travel One.

For older readers, there is of course the highly successful company, Saga.

So whatever you fancy, there's a way to do it. Whether you want to go horse riding, diving, laze by a pool, go on structured city breaks, unstructured vacations to the Mediterranean, a singles cruise or a Caribbean spa, you can do it all, so long as you've got the inclination, the time and the dosh.

For more details on all these suggestions, take a look at the Help Yourself Directory at the end of the book.

Let's face it: you have no idea how long you're going to be single for. So use whatever time you have to indulge and stimulate yourself. Right now, if you don't take responsibility for having a good time – no one else is going to do it for you.

18

A New Romance?

Do you want a new romantic partner? The automatic response for most people is a resounding 'yes'. And the likelihood is that most adults will achieve this.

I can tell you from the evidence of my postbag – as well as my personal knowledge of people forming loving relationships well into pensionable age – that nowadays you're never too old to find someone new.

Once you've been on your own for a few months, it's natural that you should begin to think that new romance is possible. You'll probably also find that many of your friends are trying to get you back into the dating game. They may start arranging for you to meet other divorced or single individuals – and some of their arrangements could feel a bit heavy-handed! You might find that when you turn up for dinner with old friends, you'll be seated next to someone of the opposite sex who your pals think could be perfect for you. Of course, sometimes they're right – but more often they're not.

Dating again can be fun – and it should be. But my advice to you at this stage is to try to keep things frivolous – and not to go looking for a long-term relationship, or marriage.

For a start, it's unlikely that you're really ready for something permanent. Secondly, I think this is a good time to ask yourself whether you really do want a new long-term partner? Or whether you just *think* you should have one, because you always *have* had one, or because you've always assumed that life is better when you're part of a couple than when you're single?

If you've taken the lessons of Chapter Seventeen to heart, by now you should be fully engaged in enjoying your single life and in doing new things and meeting new people – and I hope this is helping you to feel really good about yourself.

This single living is good for your recovery. And time and again I have seen people who have really thrown themselves into being single – and who have then, when they least expected or needed it, met the partner of their dreams. This is the best way to go about things.

Sadly, many individuals who've been dumped never go through the 'embracing the single-life' phase. Neither do they get into a 'dating for fun' scenario. No, they go looking, right away, for a replacement, serious long-term partner. This is usually a recipe for disaster.

So, let's have a think about what you want and what would be good for you. You've almost certainly come through a hell of a lot of pain and suffering, and being totally honest with yourself can be a way forward to a kind of contentment in the future that has been little more than a dream up till now.

And that contentment, surprisingly, may not necessarily involve a permanent partner – at least not for quite a while. You see, if you stop yourself from racing headlong into another serious relationship and, instead, start assessing what you really want from the next ten years or so, you may decide that you don't want to totally share your life with anyone again. Or that you want to devote the next few years to your job, or to your family.

So I'd like you to look at the questions below and to tick the one which seems closest to your main reason for wanting a new and long-term relationship:

1 Do you want a partner because you're desperate to have children?

2 Do you want someone in your life, so that you'll have someone to do everything with?

3 Do you want a relationship so that you can have sex?

4 Do you want a relationship because you believe it's impossible to be happy without one?

5 Do you want someone to come into your life to make you happy?

6 Do you want a relationship because you seek financial security?

7 Do you want a relationship because you're lonely?

8 Do you want a relationship because you need someone in your life to do technical things for you – like programme the video or change plugs?

9 Do you want a relationship because you want to look after someone – cook, mend, etc.?

10 Do you want a relationship because you want someone to cook for you and to do your laundry?

11 Do you want a relationship so that you'll be looked after in old age?

12 Do you want a relationship only if absolutely the right person comes into your life: someone you love and who loves you in return?

If you've answered 'yes' to question 12, I'd like to congratulate you – because this is the only 'right' answer! Certainly it is the one that shows you to be most mentally and emotionally healthy.

So let's take the others one by one.

You want a relationship because you are desperate to have children

This is an answer generally favoured by women in their mid-thirties, though some younger women and a fair smattering of men choose it too.

I've written at some length in earlier chapters about people who have been desperate to be parents and who have gone looking – in great anxiety and fervour – for someone to provide the egg or the sperm. Such relationships do not tend to work unless both parties have exactly the same pressing agenda – and not much in the way of other needs from each other. It is possible, of course, to achieve this, but plenty of adults don't. I don't think, by the way, that it is necessarily a bad thing to get involved with someone for the express purposes of having a child, so long as your partner *knows* that this is the driving force behind the relationship.

What I see all too often is a situation where one party has been desperate to have a child and has not been truthful with the other about that desperation. Any relationship that is forged amid that kind of duplicity is unlikely to succeed. And I believe it to be immoral, as well as an abuse of trust.

If you're so desperate to be a parent, there are ways these days in which you can achieve this without deception.

You may well believe that donor insemination, using the sperm of a willing friend, or getting an obliging woman to carry your child are far less preferable to being in a wonderful relationship that makes babies the normal way – and I agree with you. But the fact is that these things are possible now. And men and women are doing them – formally and informally – all the time.

You want a partner so you'll have someone to do things with

What you're looking for here is companionship. You don't need a partner, you need an active social life.

You want a partner for sex

Obviously, to have good sex with someone else, you do need to find a compliant and lusty adult. But again, no one should embark on a serious one-to-one relationship purely for the sex, unless that basis of the relationship is understood and agreed by both parties.

If you miss having sex – and who can blame you – then be honest about it. It's not unusual nowadays for people of both genders to want uninvolved sex – and so long as you are practising safe sex and not duping anyone, this can work well for a time.

Unfortunately, sex can be a risky activity. And one of the greatest risks is emotional attachment. If people have 'uninvolved' sex on a regular basis – then frequently one or other of the participants *becomes* involved emotionally.

For this reason, if all you want is sexual relief at this time in your life, you'd be far better off concentrating on masturbation. You can invite anyone into your bed that way – courtesy of your fantasies – and it's the safest form of sex that there is. Also, you can learn a lot about your own sexual response by loving yourself and time spent in this kind of research is rarely wasted!

If you're a woman, I suggest you visit the sexual mail order websites that I've listed in the Help Yourself Directory. These companies are run by women – for women. Their belief is that women should be having a good time in bed whether they're in a relationship or not. So even if you're having sex for one, that doesn't mean it has to be monotonous – treat yourself to a toy or a book, or a video that will add variety to your solo diet.

You want a relationship because you can't be happy without one

If this is your reason, then I have to admit to failure! I have clearly failed to persuade you that life can be just as viable as a single person as it is for couples. If you genuinely hold this view, please read a couple of books on self-esteem.

You want someone to come into your life to *make* you happy

Again, if this is what you believe, I am sorry that, so far, I have not persuaded you that happiness comes from taking responsibility for it yourself. Believe me, you are always going to be disappointed if you think that your happiness depends on someone else.

You want a relationship for financial security

Is this *really* a good enough reason to seek out a new relationship? No. Gone are the days, in my opinion, when anyone should expect to be 'kept'. Of course, a good and happy relationship with the right person often does increase an individual's financial security. But adults who go looking for financial security as their prime reason for getting into a relationship are rarely happy for long. I've known several women who set out to marry rich men – and achieved their goal. None of them is happy or contented. They look waspish and nervy – despite being elegantly coiffed, designer-dressed and often dripping with diamond rings. Such people sell their soul for a platinum credit card and they find that no matter how indulged they are, their relationship is a pretty vapid experience unless it also includes love, care and respect.

Maybe you don't want a partner to make you very rich, but you do want one to help you achieve the dream of buying a Georgian house, or moving to the seaside or to a classier part of town. But the truth is that if these sorts of things are your main aim, you can achieve them without being in a relationship.

Plenty of adults *make* them happen by sharing with a sibling, or a friend, or by downsizing their home in town so that they can afford to rent a small flat for weekends by the sea.

Just because you are single for now, should not mean that you live in limbo. And people who take steps to achieve the things that most matter to them, find great personal satisfaction in what they've been able to do for themselves.

And what tends to happen is that, having put effort into making the changes they want to see in their lives, they do then attract a partner – because they are energetic, enthusiastic and dynamic, which are all characteristics that most of us find compelling.

You want a relationship because you're lonely

Get out there and build a social life – and soon you won't be.

You want a relationship so you'll have someone to do technical things, like mending plugs

Are you serious? If you want a handyman – hire one!

You want to have someone to look after

It's not a partner you want – it's a pet. Go out and get a cat or a dog, or a budgie.

You want someone to cook and mend for you

Shame on you – in this day and age, too! You need a house-keeper, not a lover.

You want a partner so you'll have someone to care for you in your dotage

Beware of such thinking. You might marry someone years younger than you, but you can never guarantee the result you want. Your partner may walk out – tired of being a nursemaid. He or she may get a terminal illness, like cancer or Alzheimer's, leaving you as the carer. No one can predict the future, so rethink your aims.

Now, I'm not saying that most of us don't gain all sorts of bonuses when we find someone to love – someone who eventually becomes our new partner for life. All I am saying is that, for real happiness, you need a relationship that's based on most of the following:

- love;
- respect;
- companionship;
- compatibility.

Of course, if you can get all these and also get wealth, or children, or a handyman, or a great cook too, then you're *really* laughing!

Get thinking about what you really want, and don't simply assume that your next stage must be to have a new, permanent partner. Do you really want someone full-time with all the uncertainties and compromise that that entails? Or can you achieve what you most want in other ways? It's a good thing to find out – before you go any further.

19

What to Avoid When You Start Dating Again

After reading Chapter Eighteen, you may be rethinking your priorities, just like one of my former clients did.

She dealt with her heartbreak, and then surprised herself by how much she started enjoying her new, single life.

She told me: 'Do you know, I assumed when my marriage broke up – and I was so devastated – that the only thing that would make me feel better would be to find a new, long-term relationship. But now, I'm not so sure. I think I need more time just for me. I'm enjoying my own space. For the first time in my life, I'm discovering myself and putting myself first.'

This kind of thinking frequently crops up in people who take their time over their heartbreak, and who look after themselves properly rather than get straight back to seeking someone special. Most commonly, women who have been married for a long time get a real taste for solo life. Some men, too, start thinking that after all the years of mortgages and bringing up children and propping up less than perfect relationships, it's time they pleased themselves.

So, if this is the way your instinct is taking you – go with it. Plenty of other adults are obviously thinking and feeling the same. The burgeoning amount of single households bears witness to this fact: and there is no evidence these days to suggest that all these single people are sad, dysfunctional individuals craving 'coupledom'! Far from it.

Just one note of caution: don't get too solitary. Make sure that your new interests also involve enlarging your circle of friends. The chances are that the demise of your relationship ended some mutual friendships, so you should be bumping up the numbers of your network of support. This is something we all need to do.

But what if, as part of your single life, you'd also like to go dating? You might feel quite nervous about this – especially if you were with your former partner for a long time. In the next chapter, I'll be focusing on the modern ways of meeting potential partners, but before that, let's have a think about what you may want to *avoid*.

As I have said before, the first thing is to avoid getting too serious too soon. After all, you're just emerging from a period of great pain. So when you start dating, try to be light-hearted about it. Try to have a good time. Try to meet different types of people if possible – and try to be open to the idea of having dates with some individuals whom you may never have considered before.

If one of these fun pairings turns out to have the potential to become long-term and exclusive, then that will be great. But I don't think that, at the moment, your top priority should be to find that one very special person. Instead, give yourself some time to play the field.

Apart from being a jolly experience, this period could be very useful to you in breaking old patterns which have frequently proved to be destructive ones.

Now, some readers may only have had one or two relationships and they may be confident that once they've got over their heartache, they can go on to find a new and healthy romance. If you fall into this category, that's fine. But many other people will look back and see a catalogue of disasters. If this is true of you, then it could be very useful at this stage in your life to try to assess what tends to go wrong and to attempt to put it right.

So, do you seem to find the same flaws in your partners time and time again – even though at first they all seemed to be ideal, or completely different from previous lovers?

The fact is that many of us do repeat the same mistakes – until we *recognise* that we do, and take steps to look for different partners in the future. A lot of this has to do with our parents.

I don't want to get heavy about this, particularly since this book is not designed to go into immense detail about people's parenting. There are plenty of books that do; and if at this point in your development you feel that you need to understand your childhood better in order to understand yourself as an adult, then a quick glance at any of the major Internet book-stores will provide you with a huge range of suitable titles. Some of the recommended books in the Help Yourself Directory at the back of *this* book will benefit you too.

As well as books, there are plenty of counsellors and therapists who are skilled in assisting adults to come to terms with their upbringing – and this may not be a bad time to consider having some professional help.

On the other hand, you may well be able to help yourself – at least to some extent. Often, just accepting that we have a tendency to go for certain types alerts us to what we've done in the past, and opens our minds to other possibilities.

Fiona, for example, has always gone for 'mad, bad and dangerous to know' blokes. She's aware that their twinkling eyes and seductive touch have broken hearts before, but each time she hopes to find happiness. Fiona has been hooked on a type.

If she is to build an equal, loving relationship, she needs to widen her horizons. It's not easy, but she's beginning to give other kinds of men a chance, and she's tried dating completely different guys from those she would normally have gone for. She's currently dating a quiet Scotsman. He doesn't have the gift of the gab like her usual choices, but she's starting to see that he is a decent, honest guy with whom she may have a future.

Lisa's into men who need looking after. Unlike Fiona, she did not reframe her ideas after her last relationship and now she's not only found herself yet another lame duck, unfortunately she's married him too.

Lisa has a high-powered television career. Her new husband has opted to give up his job so that he can write a novel. The trouble is that – after five months of doing nothing – he hasn't even got round to starting it. Lisa can't believe that she's landed herself with yet another guy who's sponging off her. She only got married again because she wanted a baby. But the truth is that she's got one at home already – and he's becoming less cute by the day. 'I wish I'd broken my pattern before I got into this marriage,' she says.

Meanwhile, Maureen has always been attracted to childish toyboys; Flora's men always turn out to be violent; Sandra has had a string of men who put her down and who never bother with her except when they want sex; and as for Patti, all her men have been married to other people – for the simple reason that these guys feed her view of herself that she isn't very lovable or worthwhile and therefore isn't likely to attract someone who'll put her first.

Fortunately, things are eventually changing for Patti. After her last affair, she decided that it was time to build up her self-esteem. So she's been reading some books on the subject and she's also enrolled in a local assertiveness class.

'It's early days,' she says, 'but I hope I'm now going to stop making myself available to blokes who can never be fully available to me. I can't say I don't know the signs. I could spot them a mile off! And I want to stop believing that having a part-time partner is the best I can expect.'

All these women want to break with their usual patterns. And they're going to try to do so by examining their pasts and by trying to go out with men who are different from their usual choices.

But it isn't just women who fall into the same patterns time after time.

Brian would love to have a relationship with an easygoing, gentle woman but keeps picking females who are critical of his attitudes and his looks. His mother was a cold but very capable person. And he can see that he tends to seek out women just like her, even though they are not what he wants. So for now, he's decided to avoid going out with any teachers or nurses! He tells me that women in these professions are 'often on the bossy side' – and they remind him of his mother. So right now he's going out with a hairdresser, who is an older, relaxed and very jolly woman who seems to thrive on chaos.

'I wouldn't normally have even looked at someone like Greta,' he told me. 'But I've realised that by casting my net wider, I'm giving myself a chance to find happiness.'

Then there's Gavin. In the past he always got involved with petite women who collected soft toys and read magazines rather than books. Time and again, he found himself with this kind of woman because he fancies her type physically. And it's probably no accident that he comes from a family where the mother was what he calls 'a rather fluffy type' who left all the decisions in the home to his father and never stretched her brain.

It's also unlikely to be a coincidence that Barry has always felt that a man should provide for his mate and should be brighter than she is, and more able in every department. But after thinking about it long and hard, Barry's decided that he would like a more grown-up relationship with an intelligent woman who has views of her own – even if these challenge his own. So he is currently dating someone with a better degree than his own who is actually making more money than he is.

'I'm not sure I'm going to be comfortable with this long-term,' he tells me, 'but seeing someone so different has opened my eyes to the fact that the world is full of fascinating females of all types – and I was restricting myself to just one.' If you suspect that you're like these men and women, in that you've continually dated the same type, why not make this the time when you will widen your choice, and have a go at meeting people who are totally different to those in your past.

But what if you've had a string of unsuccessful relationships that seem to you to all have been entirely different – apart from the fact that they didn't work out? In this situation, it can help to draw up a plan of the characteristics of all your past boyfriends, girlfriends or spouses.

Take a sheet of A4 paper and turn it sideways. Next, from the left, draw as many columns as there have been significant partners in your life. Put their names at the head of each column. Then write down all the characteristics you can remember about the first one – good and bad. Then list the characteristics of your second partner, and so on, till you've covered them all.

When you've finished, take a different colour pen and circle each characteristic you've *valued* in these people. When you've done that, select another colour pen and draw a square round all the characteristics that you *disliked* – and that created pain and problems for you.

Almost certainly you'll find that the same traits – positive as well as negative – turn up time and time again.

If you've worked through this book doing all the tasks suggested, you will already have completed lists of what was good and bad in your most *recent* relationship (see Chapters Eleven and Twelve), so there may not be too many surprises about him or her. But what *may* surprise you is how many similarities there have been in your other romances.

This exercise won't instantly cure you of wanting the same kind of partner – but it should alert you to what you keep doing to yourself. And once you're aware of it, you should be able to avoid doing it and instead to try something different.

Finally, are there any types of dates that you should definitely avoid at all costs? Well, there are some but, unfortunately, you're unlikely to spot them till you've been out with them at least once. But in general, you should avoid anyone who is not in control of his or her drinking or drug use – or anyone who is a compulsive gambler. Of course people can change, but you've been through a lot already, and I would advise you not to get involved right now with anyone who has more problems than you do.

Individuals who get unreasonably angry are not a good bet either. Neither, obviously, are men or women who resort to physical violence. Getting involved with someone who treats you badly will demean you at a time when you should be building your self-esteem and looking for a varied and enjoyable social life. People who put up with this kind of bad treatment are in effect saying to the world, and to themselves, that they don't value themselves and that any relationship is better than no relationship. And I hope that no one who has read this book right through to this chapter believes that there is any truth in such thinking.

Lastly, please don't put up with shoddy treatment sexually. It's important to protect yourself from infection and – if you're young enough – from unwanted pregnancy. Carefree dating can only be achieved if you're practising safe sex. And if you meet someone who's not prepared to practise this with you, then don't have sex with that person. Also, don't put up with selfishness or ignorance in bed. Maybe your last relationship wasn't too hot between the sheets. Well, don't repeat that experience.

If, for example, you're a man whose previous partner was ungenerous or very inhibited – and you longed for something better – then don't short-change yourself again. And no woman nowadays should allow herself to get stuck with a guy who thinks that a woman should be grateful if she's getting laid – no matter how badly. Those 'roll-on, roll-off' Romeos should be given the boot!

Today's woman should expect a lover who understands about love-play and tenderness – and about how to help women achieve satisfaction in bed. There are literally hundreds of books which explain the sexual workings and responses of us females, so there's no excuse for any guy to act like a caveman.

So, as you start dating again, be adventurous in your outlook and get back out into the dating game with enthusiasm. But remember that this should be fun. So, if you meet someone who feels like really hard work, or who puts you down, or doesn't appreciate you, then don't put up with it. Move on.

You've come a long way. You've overcome much heartache, so don't get in a position where you're likely to experience more.

20

Twenty-First-Century Dating

After the last two chapters, I imagine you have some idea now about what you'd like to avoid in any new relationship. And if you have started dating again, I hope you're having a good time experimenting with different kinds of people.

But, supposing you've been out of your relationship for over six months, and you're ready to start dating, but so far it hasn't happened. How should you go about it?

The traditional method is to meet someone through your current circle of friends, family and work colleagues. And this is still an excellent way to go about it. In fact, it's most people's preferred route to romance. In a BBC survey of four thousand single people aged between seventeen and seventy, conducted at the end of 2002, 88 per cent of the respondents said that they favoured this way of meeting potential partners.

But your circle may be:

- small;
- depleted by the break-up of your previous relationship;

- mainly comprised of other couples who don't have many single friends.

If this is the case, you need to try something else – especially if your work-place is not likely to provide you with good dating material either. A lot of adults work with colleagues who are nearly all of the same gender as themselves. This may be great if you're gay, but not much help otherwise!

So, if you're not getting dates through work, or through your friends, you need to play the Numbers Game. This involves you using your leisure time to meet large *numbers* of new people.

Obviously, going fishing alone for ten hours on a Saturday may be soothing, but it's unlikely to provide you with a new relationship. So you need to do your homework and to get involved in the sort of sociable activities that might bring you romance.

I'm told that Salsa classes are packed full of single women and gay men. So if you're a woman looking for a mate, this isn't likely to be very fertile hunting ground But if you're a bloke – of whatever persuasion – you should be spoilt for choice!

On the other hand, women are almost bound to meet eligible men at rugby, athletics and tennis clubs – and also at the gym. In all of these places, men generally outnumber women. And the men are often unattached – which is why they have all that time to play sport!

A single friend of mine who is interested in art says that lectures on painting at places like the National Gallery are packed full of interesting individuals of all ages and types.

And Ceroc, the very trendy jiving organisation, is a great way to meet a partner. I have a friend who's met her fiancé that way. And she personally knows lots of people who have got hitched as a result of meeting over a hot dance floor.

So, if you're looking to get back to dating, use your leisure time wisely and you'll almost certainly get results.

If you don't, there are lots of other ways to try.

Personal (Lonely Hearts) Ads

For decades these were seen as 'sad' or as a last resort, but not any more. Nowadays, really capable, attractive and intelligent adults use them. They are a particularly good way of meeting people if you aren't computer-literate and don't want to try Internet dating.

Nowadays, most regional and local papers have these kinds of ads. So do the Nationals. And it makes good sense to advertise – or to reply to ads – in a paper you normally read. An *Independent* reader isn't, for example, likely to find a soulmate from the *Daily Telegraph* – or vice versa.

Talking of the *Daily Telegraph* – I heard a lovely story the other day about a couple who found love from advertising in their Kindred Spirits column. At their wedding reception, they displayed a giant copy of the ad that had brought them together! How refreshingly frank that is – and it shows how the stigma attached to 'lonely hearts' ads has largely disappeared.

If you live in London, the *Evening Standard* is worth trying. They include personal ads on three days of the week. And the stakes look good if you're female as there are only 445,000 female readers to 612,000 males! *Time Out* is also a good magazine to try.

All reputable publications offer guidelines on safety if you meet up with someone – and you should always observe them. These generally include:

- let someone else know where you're going on a first date;
- meet in a public place;
- get there by using your own transport rather than accepting a lift.

Internet Dating

This has really taken off in the last year or so. In fact, I don't think I know an unattached adult who has not tried one or two of the very many sites that are available!

Obviously, new sites are launching all the time, but I have asked various people to let me know about their favourites and I'm going to share their preferences with you, but you shouldn't take any mention in this book as a strong recommendation from me. Neither would I want you to think that there is any implied criticism of any sites I've failed to mention. I've simply included those that my clients, and my single friends and colleagues, have recommended. Further details of any company mentioned can be found in the Help Yourself Directory at the back of the book.

But why do people use Internet dating services? In a survey conducted by *Loot* two years ago, over 30 per cent said that the Internet 'saves time' in meeting new people. And almost 12 per cent of them believed that selecting someone over the Internet 'avoids unnecessary confusion and misunderstanding'.

You might also be interested to know that 65 per cent of the respondents to that survey who used Internet dating had been educated to degree level or above – and that over a third of them were earning in excess of £30,000 a year.

The Internet also favours individuals who are not necessarily very confident and chatty. Internet dating gives you a chance to discuss yourself and your needs and wants in as leisurely a way as you want. And, assuming that most people are honest, you can rule out many 'waste-of-time' contacts by finding out quite a lot about potential partners before you ever meet them.

As a very elegant, accomplished thirty-something friend said to me recently: 'I went on a blind date the other evening, which was absolutely ghastly. And I suddenly realised that I knew far less about this person than if I'd found him on the Web. So I'm sticking with the Internet from now on!'

Everyone, it seems, has their Internet favourites. One of my clients, who's into green issues and is a non-smoker, is very keen on an organisation called Natural Friends.

A colleague, who is half-Jewish, enjoys the site called Jewish Singles and finds the choice of men there – of all ages – very interesting. She also feels that she is being true to her roots.

A Sikh friend who has had European and Sikh boyfriends – having refused to go through the traditional arranged marriage that her family would have preferred – thinks that Soul Sikhers is a good site, with plenty of choice among people who have been brought up and educated in Europe.

Barry, a single man who is emerging from a broken love affair, is especially keen on Dating Direct, because it is a UK service and he feels that the people who join it are a bit more serious about finding a partner than they are on some other sites.

Match.com is one of the market leaders and Chrissie, a divorcee from Surrey, thinks it's fun and easy to use. 'This service is attractive to people of all ages and types,' she tells me. 'If you want to date a Frenchman living in France, for example, you can find one. In fact it's easy to meet up with people all over the world, which is good if you have a yen to travel, or if you've always hankered after an Italian lover, or something exotic like that.'

Worldwide, Match.com claims to have 140,000 registrations a week. The company's been going since 1995 and by March of 1996, the first baby of a Match.com-inspired marriage was born. Since then there have been at least 50 more babies and more than 1300 marriages.

Margaret, a client of mine who is a Londoner and a divorcee in her forties, favours the site called Love and Friends. Margaret has only recently learned to use the Internet, and she found this site very easy to cope with and 'rather friendly and British'. She told me: 'You can actually use quite a lot of the site as a free member. You can certainly see the types of people who are signed up on it – and even an Internet novice like me can understand how it all works.'

Date.com is another of the American-owned dating sites. It claims to have two million users worldwide – and says that fifty marriages took place among its users in the past year. Millie – a thirty-five-year-old nurse – told me it was easy to use, and that it would appeal to people from all social groups. But she felt that although the basic service was free, you don't get much for that. For full benefits you need Gold Membership.

Finally, Udate.com is hugely popular and claims to be the Number One online romance and relationship site for the over twenty-fives. Globally, six thousand people join the organisation every day. Fran, an old friend of mine, finds the site very exciting but, as with many other websites, she has discovered that the 'free' membership gets you very little. 'You can see the goodies,' she told me, 'but you can't touch without parting with cash.'

Speed Dating

This is the newest short-cut to dating so far. Basically, you go along to an evening where there are an identical number of men and women – usually about twenty of each. The UK events started in London but now take place in several British cities.

Some of the events are organised specifically for certain groups of individuals like City professionals, or media and creative workers, journalists, or Asian men and women.

What happens is that the women all sit at individual tables and the men circulate every time the bell rings – which is about every three minutes. In other words, you have a very short time with each potential partner. But people who've tried it tell me that it's long enough to determine whether or not there's a spark between you.

You don't have to reject anyone face-to-face. If you want to meet someone again, you tick a box on a piece of paper – and if he or she feels the same, the organisers will put you in touch with each other later.

For someone who's been out of the dating scene for a while, speed dating can feel quite scary. On the other hand, after just one evening, you might go home with several possible dates.

One way of plucking up courage to try it, is to book up with a friend of the same gender. Then you'll have someone to compare notes with and have a laugh with – even if you hate it or it doesn't work for you.

Introduction Agencies

If you are especially keen to find a long-term partner, you may come to the conclusion that you should enrol in an Introduction Agency. Many of these agencies now have websites, so finding out about them is probably easier than it used to be.

But there are one or two points to bear in mind:

1   You should choose an agency that is a member of the Association of British Introduction Agencies (ABIA). These agencies follow strict guidelines and should any of them ever go out of business, your membership will be transferred, free of charge, to another member agency that offers a similar service.
2   You should be specific about what you want, and you should ask exactly what they can offer you.
3   Don't assume that the most expensive agency is the best.
4   Don't be put off if the agency asks for lots of identification. They want to be sure whom they're dealing with. And it's vital that there are measures in place to preserve clients' safety, security and confidentiality.

Below, you will find a list of some of the best-known agencies, all of which are in business at the time of writing. (Their contact details are in the Directory at the back of the book.) But this list is here simply as an aid for you to make your own choice. I am not endorsing or recommending any of them specifically.

What I do urge you to do – especially before you sign up with any introduction agency and part with any money – is to take a look at the website called Which Intro.

Which Intro is an organisation, linked to Single Living, which aims to guide adults into making a good choice when they decide to embark on the Introduction Agency route.

Affinity

This agency was set up in 2000 and is aimed at professional people. It covers London and the Home Counties.

Best of Friends

This company prides itself on offering a safe, confidential and caring service to clients in Shropshire, the West Midlands and Mid-Wales.

Classical Partners

Aimed at professional adults who love classical music and conversation, it claims to attract cultured, educated and interesting people from the UK, Europe and the US. It offers both a social membership – visits to concerts etc. – and one involving introductions to other members. Diane Walters, Director of Classical Partners, firmly believes that 'music is the food of love'.

Connections

This is a well-established agency with a good reputation and is based in the East Midlands. Connections believes in 'treating people as individuals' and there is no use of computers in the matching process.

Drawing Down the Moon

Established in 1984, this agency is mainly for graduates from the business, professional and creative worlds who are seeking long-term relationships.

Executive Club of St James

This is a very exclusive agency. Members must fall into the age group of 22–58 for men, and 26–52 for women. The organisation only accepts professional people and the expectation is that they will be intelligent, articulate, well-mannered and socially skilled. Clients are interviewed for 2–3 hours before being accepted.

Initial Approach

This agency is aimed at people living in Scotland. The emphasis is on enjoying life and meeting like-minded Scots. The proprietor tells me that they have a successful approach and average ten weddings a year among their members.

Julie Rayner

Established in 1984, this is the largest agency in the Midlands. Everyone is welcome – unless they are assessed as being not emotionally ready to join.

Kids No Object

This agency has been going since 1986. It caters for family-oriented singles, aged 20–55, from all walks of life. The client base is mainly from London and the South East.

Sara Eden

This is another agency serving London and the Home

Counties. Clients are personally matched. The agency also arranges social events. Their clients are usually busy, professional people, who are serious about finding a relationship.

The Right Method For You

There are so many ways of meeting new partners nowadays that it would be difficult to say which is the right way for you. With such a choice, you might start one way, and progress to another.

Crucially, British adults are much more confident about meeting partners through ads, agencies or the Internet and any stigma attached to these methods has now largely gone. There is every chance, therefore, that no matter what your age, you can find someone special with whom to share your life. But don't forget the most important lesson of this book which is that in order to find love, you first should love and value yourself.

21

If You Can Love Once, You Can Love Again

You may be reading this chapter having had the book for several months – and having worked through it page by page, trying to act upon its advice. I hope you are feeling much better now – and that you are looking forward to the rest of your life.

On the other hand, you may have read through to the end of the book in a matter of days, or even hours. Your heart may be newly broken. You may be looking for answers – quick answers, maybe. Unfortunately, there aren't any quick answers. Recovery is usually a lengthy business – but one that *can* be achieved.

Whatever stage you've reached in your recovery, please accept that love of another person is a kind and noble and generous thing. And that people who love once, can love again. Indeed, a broken heart is often the price we pay for learning important stuff about ourselves and other people – and is an excellent preparation for finding a future happy relationship.

I do hope as you reach these last pages of the book that you are feeling much more optimistic than when you read the *first* one, and that you will one day look back on your suffering without regret.

As Tennyson wrote (and nineteenth-century poets knew a thing or two about heartbreak):

> *'Tis better to have loved and lost*
> *Than never to have loved at all.*

The Help Yourself Directory

Books

Nick Ball & Nick Hough, *The Sleep Solution* (Vermilion, 1999)

Julia Cole, *After the Affair* (Vermilion, 2001)

Julia Cole, *Loving Yourself, Loving Another* (Vermilion, 2001)

Jill Curtis, *Find Your Way Through Divorce* (Hodder and Stoughton, 2001)

Anne Dickson, *A Voice For Now* (Piatkus, 2003)

Windy Dryden & Colin Feltham, *Counselling and Psychotherapy* (Sheldon Insight, 1995)

Suzie Hayman, *Relate – Moving On: Breaking Up Without Breaking Down* (Vermilion, 2001)

Harville Hendrix, *Getting the Love You Want* (Owl Books, 2001)

Virginia Ironside, *You'll Get Over It* (Hamish Hamilton, 1997)

Andrea Kon, *How to Survive Bereavement* (Hodder and Stoughton, 2002)

Tony Lake, *Living With Grief* (Sheldon Press, 1984)

Gael Lindenfield, *Assert Yourself* (HarperCollins, 2001)

Gael Lindenfield, *Managing Anger* (HarperCollins, 2000)

Liz Simpson, *Get a Single Life* (Hodder and Stoughton, 2001)
Christine Webber, *Get the Happiness Habit* (Hodder and Stoughton, 2000)
Christine Webber, *Get the Self-Esteem Habit* (Hodder and Stoughton, 2002)

Support Organisations and Other Useful Websites

Depression Alliance: www.depressionalliance.org; Tel: 0207 633 0557
Families Need Fathers: www.fnf.org.uk; Tel: 0207 613 5060
Gingerbread: www.gingerbread.org.uk; Tel: 0800 018 4318
National Association for the Divorced and Separated: www.divorceandseparation.org.uk; Tel: 01692 583358
National Council for One-Parent Families: www.oneparentfamilies.org.uk; Tel: 0800 018 5026
National Phobics Society: www.phobics-society.org.uk; Tel: 0870 7700456
NetDoctor: www.netdoctor.co.uk
On Divorce: www.ondivorce.co.uk
Samaritans: www.samaritans.org.uk; Tel: 08457 909090
Single Living (formerly Single Again): www.single-living.com
So You've Been Dumped: www.soyouvebeendumped.com; Tel: 0870 742 5315

Legal and Mediation

Solicitors' Family Law Association (SFLA): www.sfla.org.uk; Tel: 01689 850227
Family Mediation Scotland: www.familymediationscotland.org.uk; Tel: 0131 558 9898
National Family Mediation: www.nfm.u-net.com; Tel: 0117 904 2825

UK College of Family Mediators: www.ukcfm.co.uk; Tel: 0117 904 7223

Assertiveness Training

Capita Learning and Development: www.capita-ld.co.uk; Tel: 0870 400 1000

Also check with your local council's education department, or with your public library for evening/day classes in assertiveness in your own area.

Free or Low-Cost Help for Sex and Relationship Problems

Brook (under 25s): www.brook.org.uk; Tel: 08000 185023

Couple Counselling Scotland: www.couplecounselling.org; Tel: 0131 558 9669

Relate: www.relate.org.uk; Tel: 0845 130 4010

Youth Access (under 25s); Tel: 0208 772 9900

Professional Organisations (Psychotherapy/Counselling)

British Association for Behavioural and Cognitive Psychotherapies: www.babcp.com; Tel: 01254 875277

British Association for Counselling and Psychotherapy: www.bacp.co.uk; Tel: 0870 4435252

British Association for Sexual and Relationship Therapy: www.basrt.org.uk; Tel: 0208 543 2707

British Association of Psychotherapists (analytical approach): www.bap-psychotherapy.org; Tel: 0208 452 9823

British Psychological Society: www.bps.org.uk; Tel: 0116 254 9568

National Council for Hypnotherapy: www.hypnotherapists. org.uk; Tel: 0800 952 0545

National Council of Psychotherapists (many psychotherapeutic approaches represented): www.natcouncilofpsychotherapists. org.uk; Tel: 0115 913 1382

United Kingdom Council for Psychotherapy: www.psycho therapy.org.uk; Tel: 0207 436 3002

Activities and Education

Ceroc: www.ceroc.com; Tel: 0208 846 8563

Department for Education and Skills: www.dfes.gov.uk; Tel: 0870 000 2288

Learn Direct: www.learndirect.co.uk

National Federation of 18-Plus Groups: www.18plus.org.uk; Tel: 01531 821210

Open University: www.open.ac.uk/firststep; Tel: 0870 900 0305

Ramblers' Association: www.ramblers.org.uk; Tel: 0207 339 8500

Travel

Friendship: www.friendshiptravel.com; Tel:0289 446 2211

Solo's Holidays: www.solosholidays.co.uk; Tel: 08700 720700

The Great Events Group: www.thegreateventsgroup.com; Tel: 08707 405055

Travel Companions (part of Single Living): www.single-living. com; Tel: 0208 762 9933

Travel One:www.travelone.co.uk; Tel: 01689 822430

Internet Dating

Date.com – major American-owned global dating site: www. date.com

Dating Direct – claims to be the UK's largest dating service: www.datingdirect.co.uk

Jewish Singles – mostly for Jewish people or for those seeking a Jewish mate: www.jdate.com

Love and Friends – the online dating service of Drawing Down the Moon: www.loveandfriends.com

Match.com – very popular worldwide site, established in 1995: www.match.com

Natural Friends – for health-conscious, non-smokers interested in 'green' issues: www.natural-friends.com

Soul Sikhers – based in Britain, providing a 'fresh approach to Sikh introductions in the modern age': www.soulsikhers.com

Udate – with six thousand people worldwide joining every day, this is a huge site: www.udate.com

Introduction Agencies

I recommend that you start by looking at Which Intro. This is a database of dating agencies in the UK, which is affiliated to the Single Living organisation: www.whichintro.com

Affinity – (London and Home Counties). Fees start from £350: www.affinitylondon.com; Tel: 0208 832 9030

Best of Friends – (Shropshire, Midlands, Mid-Wales). Fees from £20 to £600: www.bestoffriends.co.uk; Tel: 01952 814313

Classical Partners – (UK, America, Europe). Fees from £225: www.classicalpartners.co.uk; Tel: 01707 601315

Connections – (East Midlands). Fees up to £500: No website; Tel: 01773 520907

Drawing Down the Moon – (South East). Fees from £795 to £6995: www.drawingdownthemoon.co.uk; Tel: 0207 937 6263

Executive Club of St James – (London-based). Fees from £135 to £7500: www.thematchmaker.co.uk; Tel: 0207 930 5555

Initial Approach – (Scotland). Fees from £69 to £539 with monthly payments in addition: www.initial-approach.co.uk; Tel: 01786 825777

Julie Rayner – (Midlands). Fees start at £90 per year: www.julie rayner.co.uk; Tel: 01827 59515

Kids No Object – (Southern England). Fees £70 per year: www.kno.org.uk; Tel: 0870 4430 233

Sara Eden – (London and Home Counties). Fees from £677 to around £6000: www.sara-eden.co.uk; Tel: 01753 830350

Speed Dating

At the time of writing this book, Speed Dating has become very trendy. In the UK it is run by a company called Speed Dater which hosts dating events in many cities including, Birmingham, Bristol, Edinburgh, Glasgow, Cardiff, London and Newcastle: www.speeddater.co.uk; Tel: 0208 740 0011

Sex Shops For Women Online

Passion 8: www.passion8.com
Sh! Women's Erotic Emporium: www.sh-womenstore.com
Tickled (Brighton): www.tickledonline.co.uk; Tel: 01273 628725

Index